Off Grid Kid Paperback

Dale Jinks

Book Cover and Illustrations by Author

1st edition 2023

A FREE GIFT, JUST FOR YOU!

As a special thank you for purchasing this book, you can download a FREE copy of our latest outdoor activity book by scanning the QR code above.

Contents

About the Author

Dale Jinks is a UK military survival, evasion, resistance to interrogation, and extraction (SERE) instructor with around 20 years of military experience in the Royal Air Force. More importantly, he is a family man, husband to Lucy, and proud father to his two beautiful kids, Sonny and Indy.

He founded the brand 'Surviving the Kids' to inspire children all over the world to go out and discover positive experiences and create lasting memories within nature.

For more books, blog articles, and information visit the website at www.survivingthekids.com

For my inspirational kids - Sonny and Indy

You enlighten me every single day.

Chapter One

Introduction

“To raise a nature-bonded child is to raise a rebel, a dreamer, an innovator… some-one who will walk their own verdant, winding path.”

- *Nicolette Sowder*.

Let's imagine something for a moment. In a few seconds, I want you to close your eyes, and when you open them again you discover that the world around you looks very different. I want you to imagine that there is no cell phone in your pocket, no WIFI, no kitchen full of food, in fact, no roof over your head at all because you're in the middle of a forest, oh and it's raining hard! All you have are the clothes you are wearing right now. OK then, close your eyes for 5 seconds and then open them again and carry on reading, yes I actually want you to do this now. Go on.....we can't go on any further with this book until you do it.

Right perfect, thank you. How long do you think you could last alone in this new imaginary world? Where would you go to find some shelter from the rain, and how do you get yourself warm and dry again? What about when you start to feel hungry or thirsty? Would you be able to signal for help or find your way to the nearest town?

It may not seem like it anymore, but once upon a time, every man, woman, and kid lived in an entirely 'off-grid' world. No phones, no internet, no refrigerator full of fresh delicious food and ice cold drinks, not even a delivery person on a bike bringing a burger to your front door whenever you felt slightly peckish.

Back then, if you wanted something to eat, someone needed to go out and find it, or catch it, in the wild. Parents taught their children all of these cool skills because everyone in the family was expected to help out and pull their weight. For example, while dad was repairing the leaking roof, mum might be planting the seeds for crops, which meant six-year-old Johnny was out collecting the firewood that would keep everybody warm that night, while ten-year-old Sammy was hunting for rabbits in the nearby wood for the family meal later.

The modern world we live in today is very different from Johnny and Sammy's world. We have everything we need around us to keep us safe, warm, and protected. But sometimes things don't always go to plan. We can get lost or separated sometimes, and maybe you could find yourself in a situation where you're all alone with nobody else around to help.

By reading OFF GRID KID you will:

- Learn real wilderness survival skills which are taught to military troops so that they can deal with any situation at any time.

- Be challenged to make survival tools and

equipment at home, using easy-to-find items.

- Have greater confidence that if you find yourself 'off-grid', you will know exactly what you need to do and how to survive.
- Impress your family and friends with lots of new skills in bushcraft and wilderness survival.
- Know more about basic wilderness survival than pretty much 99% of the entire world.

So are you ready? Then let's get to it!

Chapter Two

Starting with your why

So WHY do you need to read this book?

You have decided to read this book, and I'm extremely pleased that you did so. However, to complete anything in this life we need to be committed and motivated. This means figuring out your **'why'**; what life skills or knowledge do you want OFF GRID KID to equip you with? I want you to take a moment now and think about what you really want to learn from this book. It could be something as simple as:

'I want to have the skills and knowledge to find wild foods to eat if I was ever lost in a forest '.

That would be a fantastic personal goal of reading this book! Another example could be:

'I want to be able to make a safe campfire at the next family camping trip, all by myself'.

These examples above, and more, you will be able to learn by diving head first into Off Grid Kid. But before we do that, I'd like you to write down 2 goals that you want to achieve from reading this book. Then once you finish reading the final page, I'd like you to flick straight back to this list you have made, to check that you've accomplished your goals!

Write your goals below:

Goal 1 –

Goal 2 –

Chapter Three

Survival Mindset

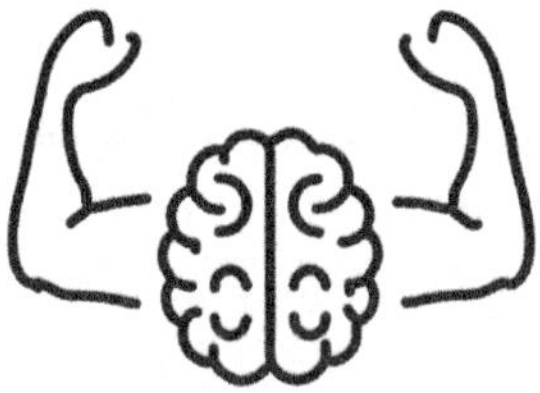

Any person who has been involved in a real-life survival situation will probably tell you that the most important thing you need to do is to keep a positive attitude. But that's easy to say in a book, and not always so easy in real life. So how can we make sure that our thoughts and mindset remain positive and helpful?

Knowledge is power

By learning from the actions and mistakes of others, we can build up a huge toolbox of knowledge that we can open up and use when we need it the most. One of my all-time favourite quotes is from the captain of US Airways Flight 1549 Chesley Sullenberger. After a flock of birds flew into and destroyed both engines shortly after takeoff, he stayed calm and safely landed the powerless and stricken jumbo jet on the Hudson River in New York, saving the lives of all men, women, and children on board. Why was Chesley able to pull off this heroic and impressive feat? Well, he was asked this very same question in an interview, and this was his reply:

> *'One way of looking at this might be that, for 42 years, I've been making small regular deposits in this bank of* ***experience, education,*** *and* ***training****, and on that day the balance was sufficient so that I could make a very large withdrawal.'*
>
> Chesley Sullenburger

In other words, the more things we can teach ourselves, the better our chances are of being able to deal with bad or unexpected events. Great news, by choosing to read this book you are in fact depositing survival education and training into your mental bank account. This is more than most of your friends and family, so well done to you!

Think like a Prepper

Preppers are people who learn skills and collect supplies so that they are ready to deal with something really bad like a natural disaster or war. They plan for the worst case, safe in the knowledge that they have everything they need to survive for months and even years. Now, I'm not saying go and build yourself an underground bunker and fill it high with canned food and solar batteries. However, we can see that by being prepared, we are less likely to find these events as scary as someone who has absolutely zero preparation and completely no idea how they are going to deal with it.

So how can you think more like a prepper? Try asking yourself more questions for starters. Questions like 'If I fell in that lake over there and needed to get warm and dry quickly, what do I have with me to start a fire?' Or how about speaking to a responsible person that you trust such as a parent or teacher about what are some of the safe things that you can eat whilst out in nature on a long hike or camping trip? You can even prepare yourself a small survival tin which you can then carry with you wherever you go. Don't worry, we'll go into survival tins and what you should put in them later in the book. Just some food for thought.

> *'Before anything else,* ***preparation*** *is the key to success.'*
>
> Alexander Graham Bell, invented the telephone

Don't worry about things you can't control

Life can be really annoying and frustrating sometimes, like when you open the bedroom curtains to see that it's raining outside, and you've planned to go to the beach that day. Or your best friend says something mean and upsetting to you at school, just because they're having a bad day and you happen to be the first person they see. The point is, this kind of thing happens all the time. The important thing to remember is that we shouldn't worry or stress about things that are out of our control. If we did, then we'd probably spend most of the day being worried, annoyed, and not much fun to be around.

As someone who is trying to survive in difficult conditions, it is crucial to have a positive mindset. This means trying your best to not worry or dwell on things you see as problems, such as it getting really cold at night or a cheeky squirrel coming along and stealing your last chocolate bar. These things are going to happen regardless of how annoyed you get, so just smile and deal with it. Instead of wasting energy being angry or upset, it's better to use that energy in thinking of a way that we can deal with the problem. So for our two little problems, here is how we might 're-frame' them:

- *Getting really cold at night* - Let's go and collect as much dry kindling and firewood as possible so that we can use the matches that we have in our survival tin to make a campfire to boil water for a sweet hot drink and help keep us warm as we sleep.

- *A squirrel steals your last chocolate bar* - We can spend a few minutes checking nearby trees and plants for berries or nuts that we know are good to eat.

If you can remember those three things; that knowledge is power, to think like a prepper, and not to sweat the things you can't control, then you will be well on your way to being able to deal with pretty much any situation that you may find yourself in.

Chapter Four

Priorities of Survival

Just like when your coach prepares you for an important playoff match in football or basketball, having a game plan will always give you an edge. It is like having a blueprint which you trust and you know that all you need to do is follow it, and everything will be alright. That's exactly how I want you to think about the priorities of survival. They are your blueprint or framework for any survival situation, and as long as you stick to them you'll do just fine.

As human beings, the things we need to live and exist are pretty simple. We need the obvious things like air to breathe, and then there are many other things like keeping our body temperature around 37°C and having water to drink so that our bodies can function properly. We all need calories from food so that our bodies can make it into fuel to power movement and brain activity, among everything else that needs powering so that we can live normal, happy lives. As you can see, these needs are all completely non-negotiable and therefore must be addressed first. If you forget to deal with these supercritical things first, then things may not go well. Your job as a survivor or someone living in extreme conditions is to make sure these areas are taken care of first. They are a priority. Then after we have taken care of the really important stuff, the other things which we may feel are important can be done.

In the British Military, there are 4 main priorities of

survival which I need you to learn like the back of your hand. If you remember nothing else from this entire book I want you to remember these 4 priorities for me. I will be testing you later in this chapter so we'll see how good your memory is, don't let me down. They are:

1. **Protection**
2. **Location**
3. **Water**
4. **Food.**

Sounds pretty simple right? Well they are supposed to be simple, that way you are more likely to remember them when it really matters. You will see that as you go further into this book, much of the information and survival guidance is organized into these four main headings. This is so that you can fully understand where that topic sits within the big four priorities of survival. We will now break each of the four priorities down and show you the kinds of things to be thinking about and why they are so important.

Protection

This is our body's first line of defence against the elements or any immediate danger that we may be in, and includes things like having shelter, giving first aid and even ensuring the clothes you have on are right for the conditions. This book will show you how to address all of the elements of protection efficiently, to ensure you can help yourself and others.

A good way to think about protection is in terms of how you'd care for a tiny baby. A newborn baby is probably the most fragile and precious example of life we can think of, just ask your parents. When a baby is born in a hospital, what is the first thing that the nurse or doctor does to protect him or her? Come on, you've seen the films. That's right, they wrap them up all snug and tight in a nice warm, fluffy blanket so they don't get cold. The nurse or doctor has immediately hit the first priority of survival, by providing some protection from the cold air. Remember, this beautiful little cutie pie was happily living in their mummy's safe and cosy 37°C womb about 30 seconds earlier, and now he or she is suddenly completely butt naked, otherwise known as being in their birthday suit, and in a relatively chilly 18°C delivery room. I guess now you can see why babies make such an almighty fuss when they are born, you can't blame them for being a bit upset.

But the first survival priority of protection covers so much more than just keeping warm. We also tend to deliver babies indoors, in a building or room, so therefore we are also providing shelter. That is a form of protection from the wind, rain, snow, and even the predators that might be lurking outside. Humans always feel safe and secure in a 'home', whether that's an apartment, a log cabin, or a simple lean-to shelter in the woods. Having a place to return to and cook food or have a wash gives an immediate lift in morale.

Back in the hospital delivery room, any medical issues are dealt with swiftly by the staff to ensure the baby is healthy and happy. You see, that's another strand of protection being addressed as first aid. But how would you cope by yourself in the wilderness if you have a wound on your leg which is bleeding badly, would you know what to do? We know that if we lose too much blood, it can be fatal; so it's important to act quickly and decisively. We'll go into much more detail in the coming chapters on everything protection.

Location

Throughout my military career, I have taught others how to 'promote their own recovery'. This means that if ever lost or separated, rather than just sitting there and hoping someone will come along and find you by pure chance, you are to actively do something to increase the likelihood of being rescued or located. This is assuming that you want to be found of course. You may be completely happy living out in the wilderness all by yourself, surrounded by trees and nature. Unfortunately, most people who find themselves lost and alone in the wilderness do need some help. Luckily we have the amazing emergency services on hand to come and find us if we somehow lose the trail during a long family hike. Using helicopters and search parties, they are well-trained to locate anyone who may be lost. However it's not easy, and most of the time it's like trying to find a needle in a haystack. That's where we can use our knowledge and skills to assist the search parties who are out looking for us. Using ordinary materials that we can find such as litter or brightly coloured vegetation, we can create bright and obvious signs that show others that we need some help. In this amazing age of technology, you can even go to a store and buy something called a Personal locator beacon or PLB's for short. At the press of a button, the PLB uses satellite constellations in outer space to send a distress signal out to emergency services with your exact location anywhere in the world. They work similarly to a Sat Nav in a car or the Maps app on your phone. Using GNSS, (Global Navigation Satellite System), once activated the PLB sends a high-frequency data burst message into space, which is then picked up by numerous satellites, before being transmitted back to a control centre on Earth. From there, the rescue mission is coordinated and within hours there can be people coming to your exact location. Well worth the small investment you could say.

So what can you do to make it easier for anyone trying to find you? How can you use items in your bag to signal the attention of aircraft overhead? What about leaving a sign on the floor which can be seen from miles away? We'll cover all of these and much more in the upcoming chapters on location.

Water

Even though this is the third priority of survival, without a supply of water to drink it is going to be near impossible to survive more than a few days. Our bodies are made up of around two-thirds of water, which seems really strange. Two-thirds is a lot, which is why water is so important to us as living creatures.

In developed countries having easy access to clean, safe drinking water is mostly taken for granted. All we need to do is grab a glass from out of the cupboard, walk over to the sink, turn the faucet and hey presto, you have water. This is certainly not the case for millions of people living in third-world countries, places in Africa and Asia where there is no access to clean running water. In fact, many children have to walk miles every day to grab a drink from the nearest well or water source. This is just everyday life for some people, and walking five, six, or maybe ten miles to bring some water for the family is often a daily chore for most children living in these places.

As a rule of thumb, it is recommended that kids

drink at least 2 litres of water per day, that's around 6-8 cups to stay hydrated. This means that your body has enough water inside it to complete all the important functions it needs to do, such as removing waste and getting oxygen-rich blood around the body. For adults, this increases up to around 3 litres for women and around 4 litres for men. If it's a really hot day and you have been sweating a lot, or you have been working really hard building a shelter to sleep in, these numbers will be much higher. Everyone knows that feeling when you get thirsty and really want a drink. Well, thirst is not a great sign of how hydrated you are. Generally, when you feel thirsty, you are already slightly dehydrated - which is when your body doesn't have quite enough water to do what it needs to do. When this happens you'll probably feel some of these mild symptoms of dehydration:

- Headache
- Easily annoyed by other people and things
- Feeling light-headed
- Dry mouth

- Finding it difficult to concentrate.

However, if you fail to recognise these early signs and symptoms or can't find any water to drink, then you could experience the more severe stages of dehydration like:

- Getting confused by normally simple tasks
- Developing a swollen tongue
- Dizziness when you stand up or move around
- Feeling very tired and not wanting to do anything
- Unable to stay awake.....until eventually…well you get it!

But don't worry, you have made the very smart decision to read this book, which means you are going to have all the skills and knowledge of a truly off-grid kid. For you, finding different places in nature where you can get water will be easy. You will even know how to make sure the water you have collected is safe to drink, and won't make you ill. But all of that is to come later.

Food

We often think of food in terms of a meal or a snack, perhaps a turkey sandwich with a few chips, or maybe an apple or an orange. But instead, I want you to think about food in terms of calories. If you have never heard of calories before, they are just a measurement of energy. If you were to lay in bed all day from morning until night watching movies or cartoons, your body would still need to use between 1500 to 2000 calories just to 'tick over'. This is because everything that happens inside your body, such as your heart beating, your lungs breathing in air, or just keeping your body heated at 37°C requires some form of energy. Even sitting down and thinking requires energy, and your brain demands around 20% of the body's total daily energy expenditure.

Food can be broken down into 4 categories, Carbohydrates, Protein, Fat and finally Vitamins and Minerals. As a survivor, we want food which will provide the highest amount of calories possible. This is because we may be busy building a shelter, collecting firewood and trying to find water to drink. All of these tasks can be very draining, therefore we need to replace the energy we are using. The best type of food for a survivor is fats, as it has the highest proportion of calories per gram. We still want carbs and protein, but their calorific content is less:

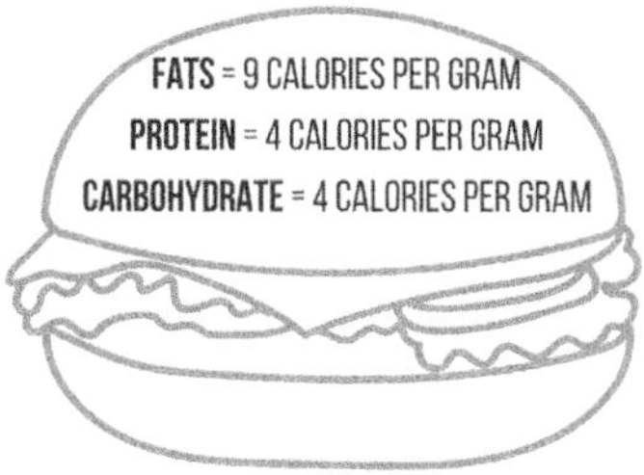

However, food is <u>not</u> a high priority for someone who is in a survival situation. That's because the human body is really good at storing energy in places like the muscles, the liver and in the form of fatty tissue. It does this whenever there is a plentiful supply of food/calories, which the body doesn't need to use as fuel right away. For example, if we sit on the couch all day watching TV or playing video games, and eat lots of calorie-rich foods like chips, chocolate and soda, more calories are coming in than being used and therefore the body will store that energy for times when there is no food around. Generally, this means we put on weight in the form of increased body fat.

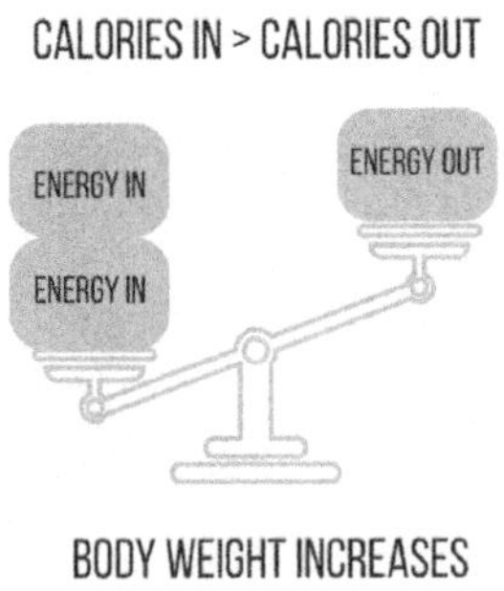

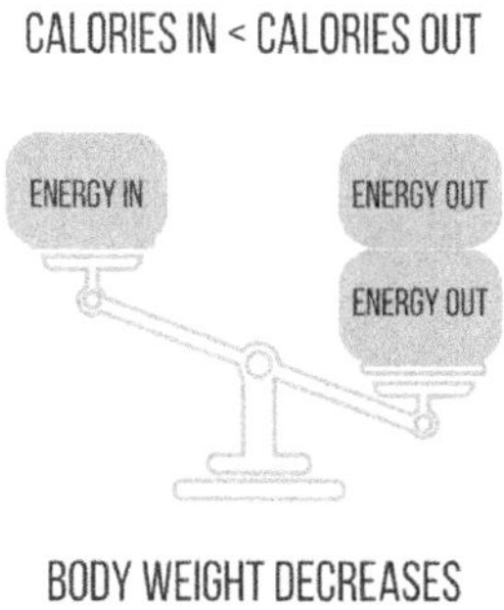

In prehistoric times, going days between meals would have been quite common, as it was not always guaranteed that a hunt would be successful. So as a species, we have evolved over many thousands of years to be really good at storing energy within the body that can be accessed if we can't find food for a while.

Of course, eventually, that store of energy will run out if we go many days without food. Once that happens, the body will start to 'eat itself' by breaking down the protein within the muscles to use as fuel. The body becomes thin, weak and more and more helpless. Without medical help, the vital organs will eventually begin to quit, and the body will shut down completely. Pretty grim hey! Remember, this is a very long process and we all have stored up energy reserves for when we really need it. Can you guess the number of days someone has gone without food and lived to tell the tale? 7 days?.....12 days?.....20 days? Believe it or not, the Guinness World Record is a whopping 382 days!

As well as calories for energy, the body also needs vitamins and minerals to work properly. Now we tend to get the majority of these from fresh fruit and vegetables. Oranges and pineapples are extremely rich in Vitamin C, which helps to support our immune system and helps us fight off harmful germs and bacteria, stopping us from getting sick. Sodium, which is salt, allows the muscles to contract and relax by ensuring nerve impulses fire properly. The list of vitamins and minerals that the body uses is very long, which is why you'll often hear people recommending we all try and eat a balanced diet. This is so that we hopefully consume as many of these important nutrients as possible.

A scottish man called Angus Barbieri went without food for 382 days, surviving only on tea, coffee, sparkling water and vitamins. He lost an incredible 276 pounds in weight.'

So you are a lone survivor, lost in the woods, or perhaps living 'off-grid' in the wilderness. What is going to be your long-term food plan? For the reasons we have mentioned above, our bodies will eventually need nutrients and calories. In this book, you will be given lots of ideas about where to look for food, how to identify edible plants and even how to build a trap to potentially snare a real survival meal.

End of Chapter Quiz

Write down your answers in pencil, then check in the back of the book to see if you're correct:

Write down the 4 Priorities of Survival:

What is normal human body temperature?

____________°C

How many calories per gram are in fat?

____________Calories

Well done, you have shown tremendous effort and you now have a greater understanding of the priorities of survival. Let's move on to the next chapter and continue this journey into the off-grid world.

Chapter Five

Making Fire

Understanding how to make and use fire is one of the things that separates us as humans from the rest of the animal kingdom. Our ancestors, cavemen and cavewomen, possibly discovered how to make fire for the first time by accident, but after this point, there was no turning back. With fire, we can warm ourselves, keep big hungry predators away from our cave and cook the food that we had hunted and gathered. Scientists believe that we first started using fire around 800,000 to 1 million years ago but it is difficult to be exact. Remains of old fire pits and simple tools have been found in regions of South Africa that date back this far. How we first discovered how to make fire is a mystery, but I'm glad we did. Because if we hadn't started using fire, then our species probably would not have evolved so successfully, and it's unlikely you or I would be here right now.

Learning how to easily make a fire is a skill that every off-grid kid needs. In this chapter I will show you how to prepare an area ready for a fire, how to find the right kind of wood and materials to burn, and some different ways you can get ignition, which means creating enough heat to light a fire.

Keep it safe

To begin with, it's a good idea to always practice your fire lighting skills with an adult present.

Here are some other important things to think about to make sure everybody stays safe:

- Before lighting, always have something close by that you can quickly put your fire out with, for example, a bucket of water, a wet towel or a spade and earth.
- Choose a good site - at least 1m away from the base of a tree and not close to any dry plants which could easily set on fire (dead grass). We do not want to start a wildfire!
- Never use any flammable liquids to help start your fire. This is always a very bad idea and never ends well.

The Fire Triangle

Unless you know this next part well, you can never truly master fire in the wild. Making fire is never an exact science, and there are so many variables that will change from one fire to the next. Therefore I want to teach you all about the fire triangle, and how this will help you to diagnose what's wrong if a fire will not light, smokes too much or goes out soon after you have lit it.

As you can see from the diagram below, the fire triangle is made up of 3 parts - Heat, Fuel and Oxygen. Let's talk about each one a little more:

Heat: Unless there is something to cause ignition, there can be no fire. When we make a fire, often we'll use a lighter or matches and this is the 'Heat' part of the fire triangle. It could also be a spark that's caused by hitting a piece of steel against some flint rock, or perhaps even an electrical spark from shorting a battery using some wire or foil. We also need to think about protecting our fire from the cold ground when we go to light it. This is why we always use a base to lay our fire bundle on before lighting, but more on this later.

Oxygen: A fire breathes air just like we do, and if there is not enough oxygen getting to the fire then it will certainly go out. Sometimes you will see people blowing at the coals of a fire to try and breathe some life if it looks like it's struggling or in danger of going out completely. When this happens, it is normally a classic sign that the fire is not getting enough oxygen or airflow to sustain a good burn. If there is very little wind, or the base of your fire sits too low in the ground, it can reduce the amount of airflow and efficiency of the burn. The best thing you can do in this situation is to move your fire to another place and try again. Try setting your fire on level ground where there is a light, steady breeze moving through the area. This should provide your fire with enough oxygen to burn the fuel that you are adding efficiently.

Another way that a fire can fail due to lack of oxygen is by adding lots of fuel too quickly, which can suffocate the fire, especially in the early stages. Having patience is important when making a fire. If you try to rush things along by adding lots of wood very quickly, there is a good chance that your poor little fire will not be able to cope and the reduced oxygen supply will cause it to gradually choke itself out. There is an art to adding the right amount of fuel to a growing fire, and this comes with a lot of practice and experience. You will learn to recognise the signs of when your fire is happily growing in energy and heat, but also when your fire needs some time before adding the next bundle of kindling or needs a gentle blow to its base to help things along.

Fuel: The best fuel for your fire is going to be dead, dry wood. You can check to see whether the wood you have found is dead by scratching off some of the outer bark. If the wood underneath looks brownish then it is most likely dead wood. It will also make a loud 'SNAP' when you break it in half. If it does not snap apart cleanly, then the wood probably still has moisture inside and should not be used. However, if the colour is a pithy green, then the wood you have is 'live', and should not be used for your fire. Live wood contains lots of moisture, which will cause the fire to produce lots of smoke and needs lots and lots of heat to burn.

Do not be tempted to try and use wet wood that has been lying on the ground to make a fire. This is not good for starting new fires, however, it may burn later on once you have managed to grow a bigger, more established fire. Ideally, you should dry out the wet wood you have gathered using heat from your fire with a simple drying rack set-up (we'll show you how to make this later). Standing deadwood is ideal for fuel for making a fire. As it is raised from the ground, it should be nice and dry on the inside, however, the outer bark may need to be removed first. You can find standing deadwood by looking for small, thin, weedy-looking trees that have not managed to get enough sunlight and died. They will feel light and brittle when you push on them, and smaller standing deadwood trees can be pushed over by hand.

Types of Firewood

Tinder: This is the material that first catches the spark and ignites quickly, giving a flame that you can then build up into an established fire. There are many different types of tinder, from man-made or synthetic items such as cotton wool and rubber to natural tinders such as silver birch bark and thin wood shavings. It is important to use a suitable, dry tinder otherwise no matter how hard you try you'll never be able to make a fire. Here are some good examples of tinder for you to try:

Natural	Synthetic
• Birch Bark • Dry, dead grass • Old Man's Beard • Birds nest • Fine wood shavings	• Char Cloth • Cotton Wool • Cotton and lint • Rubber • Candle wick

My favourite natural tinder to use in the woods is silver birch bark. It contains natural oils which act like petroleum, giving a good flame and thick black smoke. You can either light the birch bark using a flame from a match or by using sparks from a ferro rod and steel. It's always worth grabbing a few handfuls of silver birch bark for your tinder pouch if you see any whilst out on a walk in the woods.

Even rubber will ignite with a flame or spark, something like an old bicycle innertube cut into thin pieces can be used as a tinder to start your fire.

Kindling: This is the small twigs and pieces of wood which you hope will begin to burn once the tinder bundle is lit. Again, this needs to be dry dead wood which is nice and 'snappy' when you break it from the tree. Unless it is very very dry where you are, do not be tempted to use wood that has been lying on the ground as it's probably damp.

There are many different ways that you can add the kindling once the initial flame has started. My preference is to use a 'log cabin' set-up (below) which has the tinder bundle placed in between two large sticks, and then the thinner kindling is laid in a criss-cross pattern over the tinder. Once you light the tinder, the flame automatically starts to feed on the kindling above and you are away, fire! The benefits of this setup are once it's lit you don't have to worry about trying to carefully place kindling around the flame to keep feeding it, and also the spaces between the kindling mean there is lots of oxygen in the fire and it burns well.

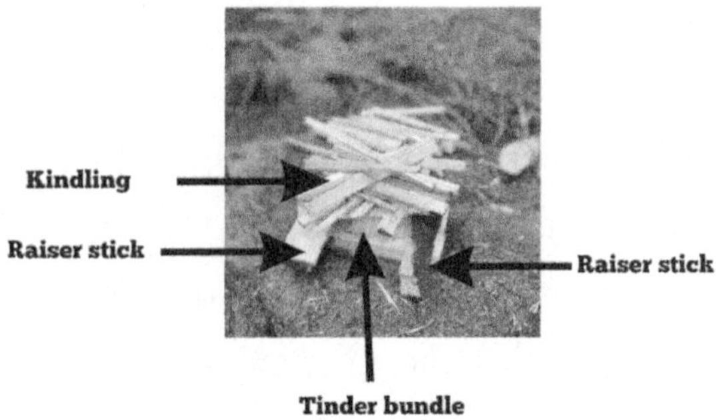

Example of a ready-made fire stack which is ready for a spark

Main Fuel: Anything larger than your kindling is known as main fuel. Once you feel that your fire has grown enough momentum from the kindling you have used, you can add larger sticks and split logs.

Be careful not to do this too early, otherwise, you risk putting the fire out. With practice and patience, you will start to learn when the fire requires main fuel just by looking at it and listening. A nice healthy fire should make 'crackling' sounds as it churns through the thin kindling fuel. Sometimes you just need to sit back and let the fire generate some heat before going in with more fuel.

The Gear System

When I explain how to gradually add fuel to a fire with our military students, I often use the example of shifting through the gears on a car like this:

- **1st gear** - You light the tinder bundle and use handfuls of the thinnest and driest kindling to slowly increase the size of the flame. Kindling that is matchstick thickness is ideal for gear 1.

- **2nd gear** - Very slightly thicker than 1st gear, no thicker than a pencil. This can be added a few sticks at a time, creating a pyramid around the flame.

- **3rd gear** - Branches and twigs which are finger thickness can be added now, the fire is looking good at this stage and is no longer in danger of going out anytime soon.

- **4th gear** - Large dead branches and split wood can be added now to really beef up the heat in the fire, great work!

- **5th gear** - Go ahead and add a log or two to your fire. Now you can sit down and admire your amazing fire or start cooking those hot dogs that you brought along for supper. Impressive fire skills, well done.

Types of fire

There are a few different ways that you can lay out a fire, depending on what the reason for the fire is. Here are the main fire lays and some advantages and disadvantages of each:

Long Fire: This is a fire that uses long branches or logs acts almost like a radiator, and is ideal for having alongside a sleeping area near to a shelter.

Advantages of a long fire:

- Heat the whole body when lying down
- Good for next to a shelter

Disadvantages of a long fire:

- Difficult to make
- Can be very time and resource-intensive

Tee-Pee Fire: This is your traditional-looking campfire, with a pyramid appearance. It's a simple but effective style of fire with multiple uses.

Advantages of a tee-pee fire:

- Easy to make
- Great for cooking on

Disadvantages of a tee-pee fire:

- Uses firewood quickly
- Heat lost upwards so not great for warmth

Star Fire: This fire gets its name because you lay long branches out in a star shape with the actual fire part in the centre. Then when the fire needs more fuel, you just push one of the 'star arms' in towards the centre.

Advantages of a star fire:

- Easy to manage and keep fed with fuel
- Simple to set up

Disadvantages of a star fire:

- Takes up lots of space, so not good for small camps
- Need to find long, dead branches

Cabin Fire: This fire set-up looks like a log cabin, with sticks stacked across one another in a neat square pattern. It's a great way to add lots of fuel to your fire and burns very well.

Advantages of a cabin fire:

- Easy to set up and add fuel once lit.
- It burns really well due to having lots of air gaps in between the wood.

Disadvantages of a cabin fire:

- You will burn through your store of firewood really quickly.
- The heat is spread out over a larger area, so not great for cooking with.

Extenders

This is something that you can add to your tinder bundle before you light the fire. The idea here is for the extender to increase the burn time of your tinder bundle, and make it less likely that the fire will fail. It gives more time to add those first few handfuls of '1st gear' kindling, slowly adding fuel and heat into the delicate early stages of the fire. It's worth having in a survival tin or your kit if you want to make fires in the wilderness.

One of the best extenders around, and certainly something I would encourage any Off Grid Kid to have in his or her survival kit is lip salve, also known as petroleum jelly. The reason why it works so well is that it's petroleum-based; as in the highly flammable liquid that you put in cars and trucks at the gas station. Just wipe a small amount onto the cotton wool, wood shavings, or whatever tinder is being used, and the flame will last much longer before it goes out.

Challenge - Try this experiment at home.....in a

safe place outside, put two identical cotton wool balls on a base, one with petroleum jelly smeared on it, and one without. Now light the two cotton balls at the same time and see what happens. How many more seconds did the extender-infused cotton ball last??

Feather Sticks

When everything is wet after it's been raining hard for a while, it can be very difficult to find good dry firewood. So what do we do? Have no fire? No, that's not an option if we want to get warm and dry out our wet clothes. Feather sticks are a great survival tool and once you know how to make them, you'll never struggle to make fire again, even in horrible wet conditions.

Firstly, you'll need to find some standing dead wood. Remember, we covered this earlier and it's the 'snappy', lightweight and brown-coloured wood which is not already lying on the floor. Thin branches which are around the size of your thumb work well or you can split thicker logs down, but this can take time and waste lots of energy. The key thing here is that underneath all of the damp, wet bark is wood that is bone dry and ready to burn. Carefully scrape away the outer wet bark using the back of your knife, as over 80% of the moisture is trapped in this outer protective layer. Moisture is not a good thing when trying to start a fire.

Now we have the wood prepared, it's time to start feathering. The aim is to create very fine ribbon curls of wood that look similar to dry, dead grass:

1. Hold the wood at the top and rest the bottom on something solid.

2. Firmly holding the knife and with a straight arm, carefully push the blade away from you and down to the base of the stick

3. Then bring your knife back to the start, rotate the wood slightly and repeat. Keep doing this until you build lots of thin, ribbon curls.

These curls make fantastic tinder and kindling for making sure your fire gets off to a good start. Have a go and challenge yourself to create the finest, curliest curls that you can. You should be able to light your feather stick just using the sparks from a ferro rod and steel. This is a skill that easily makes my all-time top 3 must-know wilderness survival hacks.

The art of making a featherstick takes practice

Primitive Methods - Fire By Friction

I'm sure you have seen a movie or TV show where somebody rubs a couple of sticks together very quickly, and after about 20 seconds there is a waft of smoke quickly followed by a raging fire. Let me tell you, in real life this process is much more difficult than it looks on TV. The aim is to make an **ember**, through the build-up of heat and wood dust. An ember is a small glowing coal which can be placed into a nest of tinder such as dry, dead grass and with some careful blowing, should burst into flames.

Here's a great way to practice fire by friction:

Bow and Drill Method:

- To make a bow and drill set you need to find a few different sticks. Firstly, you'll need to make a bow using a curved live branch which is about 3 feet long and as thick as your thumb. Cut a thin notch out of each end and tie some string or paracord between so it looks like a bow and arrow.

- Now you need a base plate, so find a dry, dead log which is around 8 inches long with a diameter of around 2 inches. Split the log lengthways to create a flattened rectangle shape which is about as thick as your thumb. Try to find some old, dead Ivy wood for this.

- Now you need a drill, which is a dry, dead branch that's perfectly straight, or as straight as possible. Hazel works really well for this. Carefully trim the drill to make a dome shape at either end.

- The cap sits on top of the drill and acts like a small handle, allowing you to create some downward pressure when spinning the wood. Use some of the Ivy wood that you collected for the base plate. You'll need to hollow out a small bowl the same size as your drill, about ½ inch from the edge of the wood.

- Twist the dowel into the bow string so it sits

tightly, then place it into the bowl you have cut into the base plate. Pressing down on top of the drill with your end cap, carefully move the bow forwards and backwards horizontally, slowly increasing the speed. Once the bowl in your base plate has become slightly deeper, carefully cut a triangular wedge shape so that the point is in the centre of the bowl. This is where your dust should collect, and hopefully your big old ember.

Now you're all set, from here it's a simple case of applying some light pressure down onto the cap whilst carefully spinning the drill to create friction and heat in the base plate. Before you know it, there should be dust collecting in your little wedge cut-out. Once you see lots of smoke coming from the dust, then you'll have an ember. Carefully place the ember in a nest of dry tinder and gently cupping the nest with your hands, giving it a long, steady blow. You should see plumes of smoke which are getting thicker and thicker until it bursts into a flame. This is one of the best feelings in the world when you make this happen for the first time, using a bow and drill set that you've made yourself. It does take a lot of practice and patience, but it's worth it. I bet there are very few adults or kids that you know, maybe none at all, who can make fire by friction. By learning the advanced skill of how to make fire without the need for matches, a lighter or flint and steel you'd certainly be in a small, select group of people.

Taking fire with you

You have a great fire at your campsite, but now you need to move to a different part of the forest or mountain. How cool would it be to be able to take some of that fire with you, and save tons of time and effort the next time you need to light a fire quickly? Well good news, there is a type of fungus called King Alfred's Cakes (also known as Coal Fungus) which allows you to transport a burning ember over long distances. They look like small black balls or pieces of coal, and you'll find them growing on dead or decaying wood, especially Ash trees. You can find King Alfred's Cakes all over the world.

Let the fungus dry out in the sunshine for a few days before using it for fire. Carefully cut the fungus in half, and you'll see it has circular rings inside. Simply light this part of the fungus using coals from your fire or sparks from a Ferro rod, and it will happily glow orange and smoulder away for hours. Then when you need a fire, all you need to do is blow on the ember inside the King Alfred's Cake to build up some heat, put it inside a nice dry nest of tinder and give it a few blows. You'll have a fire in no time.

My Top 8 Super Hacks For Making Fire

- If it doesn't go 'snap' when you break it, then don't use it for kindling.
- In wet weather, remember to strip off the bark to remove the wet stuff.
- Feather sticks are a great way of making awesome tinder/kindling when it has rained and there is no dry wood anywhere.
- Use a tee-pee fire if you're looking to do some cooking.

- Use good handful-sized bundles of 'gear 1' kindling to get your fire off to a good start. It's easy to starve your fire of fuel if you add one twig at a time.

- Choose a safe site for your fire. Do not light a fire near dry, dead grass or at the base of a tree.

- If you need to keep blowing on the fire to keep it going, then you need to think about moving it somewhere with better airflow.

- Extenders can be used to increase the chance of success when lighting a fire. Using petroleum jelly or pine resin are great examples.

Chapter Six

Protecting Yourself

Think back to the priorities of survival that we discussed earlier. Number one, numero uno, is protection - how are you going to protect yourself and others from the cold, heat, wildlife, and rain so that you can stay fit and healthy?

Clothing - Dress to survive.

Before you head out on any adventures, you need to stop and think about the climate and weather in that area. As a minimum, you should always have with you:

1. A base layer - this is a light layer next to the skin which is warm, comfortable, and breathable.

1. A mid layer - ideally a soft jacket or jumper that can trap air next to the body to keep you warm if the weather turns cold or you stop moving for a while.

1. A shell layer - is a waterproof jacket and/or bottoms that stop you from getting wet and cold if it rains. It will also help to protect you from any chilly winds if you're out in the open.

Using a layer system in this way means that you can remove something if you get too hot, and then put it back on again once you begin to feel cold. It's easy to start sweating if you are working hard building a shelter or gathering food. However, this can be dangerous for a few different reasons. Firstly, once your clothes become wet you will get cold very quickly when resting or standing still. Sweating also means that you are losing water, and need to drink more to replace what's lost. This is a huge problem somewhere like the desert, where water is very hard to find.

Basic First Aid

In everyday life, there is always a risk that we can get hurt or injured. Sometimes things just go wrong, and there is not a lot that we can do about it. If you get hurt at home, normally somebody will be there to help by maybe putting a bandaid onto a nasty cut, or maybe carrying you to an armchair if you twist your ankle. Now imagine that you are alone deep in the woods and you have a problem, would you know what to do? It's really important to learn basic medical and first aid skills which you can use if you ever find yourself lost, alone, or in a survival situation. Even if you're camping with family or out on a hike with friends, knowing the right thing to do if someone gets hurt or needs help is always impressive. In wilderness survival, being able to depend on yourself when things get tough or challenging is essential. Let's discuss some of the problems that you could face when in nature and explain how to provide suitable first aid:

Trips, slips, and falls: Far away from the urban jungle, where we walk around on completely flat sidewalks and paths all day, in nature, the ground is quite often bumpy and uneven. Tree roots are a common cause of trips and falls, so try to watch out for them as you travel through any dense woodland area. It's easy to break a bone in your wrist as you try to stop the fall using your arms.

Cuts and scrapes: Whether you are sawing branches to build a shelter or chopping up some firewood to keep warm, your chances of getting a cut or graze are quite high. Even pushing through an area of thick woodland, it's easy to scratch your arm or face on a sharp twig causing an injury. If the cut or scrape is small, then usually the body will take care of itself by forming a clot and eventually a scab. However, if it's a bad cut that is bleeding heavily, then it will need some first aid.

Blisters and sores: Not normally life-threatening, these cause pain and discomfort and are most common in the feet and hands. Walking around in wet boots all day can easily cause nasty blisters to form on the heel or toes, and makes moving around quite painful. Having damp feet and wet boots for long periods can also lead to something called *Trench Foot,* which is when the skin on the feet starts to rot and break down. This is not a good situation for any survivor and will become gradually worse unless the feet are allowed to dry properly in fresh air.

Dehydration: Earlier we described just why water is so important for our bodies. It is like the oil in a car's engine, when it gets too low everything starts to break down, and eventually, nothing will work at all. It is very easy to allow yourself to become dehydrated when working hard outside, especially on a hot, sunny day. If you feel thirsty, you are already dehydrated so do not use this as a signal of when to drink. Our bodies are constantly losing water in the form of sweat, digestion of food in the bowels, and even moisture in the air when we breathe out. So it makes sense to drink a small amount often, to replace this slow gradual loss. Someone who is becoming badly dehydrated will usually get a bad headache, be irritable, and be unable to concentrate. If things get worse, the tongue will become swollen making it hard to swallow, and the person will be unable to move.

Heat Exhaustion: This is when you get way too hot, and your body just can't keep itself at that important 37°C core temperature. When this happens, symptoms such as confusion, faintness, headaches, and nausea will be seen. Without fast action and cooling of the body, symptoms will quickly get worse. Remember to keep drinking plenty of cool water, especially on hot days as dehydration will speed up the effects of heat exhaustion. To cool itself down, the body produces sweat which makes our skin wet. As the sweat evaporates and dries, heat is removed from the body. Sometimes sweating isn't enough, especially when it's really hot or we're working the body really hard. Eventually the core temperature will simply get too high, and that's when we could start to experience problems with heat exhaustion or heat stroke.

Hypothermia: The opposite of heat exhaustion, now the core body temperature is getting too low and needs warming up. Getting wet clothes or being in cold water for too long can cause this. The body will lose heat and warmth 20 times faster in water. When the skin is wet, body heat is quickly pulled away, which is the reason we start sweating when we're too hot and need to cool down. This is a real problem at nighttime in the wilderness when the temperature is much lower. Without a fire to help us dry our clothes and increase our body temperature, hypothermia is a big risk. Things to look out for in someone who may be hypothermic are shivering, pale skin, sleepiness, and confusion.

How to deal with......

A Broken Bone: Any little trip or slip can result in a bone being broken. The tell-tale signs will be swelling and lots of pain around the area. Firstly, stop any further damage by keeping the bone still and protected. For an arm, we usually use a sling to keep the limb safely pinned against the body. You can make a sling out of any piece of material or clothing. Just make a triangle shape by folding it diagonally if it's a square, then drape it around you with the point towards the elbow. Use somebody else to tie a knot in the two ends behind the neck, not so easy if you're alone but it can be done. A break in the leg or ankle and you'll need to make some sort of splint. A splint is just a way of tying the injured part to something thin and strong like a piece of wood for example. It's impossible to walk on a broken leg, and making some 'wild crutches' could help keep you moving. Find two strong branches that are shoulder height and have a 'Y' shape at one end (you may need to cut something fresh from a nearby tree). Popping the 'Y' under your armpit, you now have perfectly good crutches to help take the weight off the broken limb.

Bleeding: The sight of blood can be worrying, especially your own. However, cuts can be really easy to treat depending on how deep or long they are. The most important thing to stop any bleeding is putting pressure on it. This will help slow the blood flow and eventually, it should stop completely after the body has created a type of 'plug' called a clot. Applying pressure right onto the wound using clean hands is fine, which will buy some time to find something more permanent such as a dressing or bandage. If you do not have a medical kit with you containing sterile dressings, then a piece of clothing or material will do the job until you receive medical assistance.

Sores and Blisters: Most of us know how it feels to have a sore or blister following a long hike in new trainers or boots. It's very uncomfortable and is felt with each step we take. The best advice is to stop blisters and sores from forming in the first place. Normally you will feel a 'hot spot' before a blister appears, and this is where the boot or clothing item is rubbing on the skin causing damage. If possible, try to identify this early and make the necessary changes. For example, if you have wet socks, now is a good time to change them for the extra pair of dry ones you have packed. This will reduce friction and stop further damage to the skin on your foot. Or perhaps it's time to stop and adjust the strap on your rucksack if you begin to feel that it is rubbing the skin around your upper back. If you do notice that a blister or sore has formed, then use clean water to wash the area and then cover it with a clean non-fluffy dressing if you have one. It's always a good idea to pack a few band-aids in a basic first-aid kit if you're planning a long hike or adventure outdoors.

Heat Exhaustion: Somebody who is feeling the effects of heat exhaustion must be cooled down quickly. This can be very serious, and it's important to identify the signs and symptoms quickly. Firstly get the person into the shade of a large tree or another object, and away from the sun's hot rays. Sit them down and be sure to remove any warm or unnecessary items of clothing. Offer some sips of cold water if you have it, and use a damp piece of fabric to wet the forehead and face. If the person is dehydrated, they may have stopped sweating which is why wetting the skin can help cool the body down. Gradually try and bring the person's body temperature down to normal, do not throw them in a cold river or lake. This sudden drop in temperature could cause more problems such as shock or heart issues.

Hypothermia: Here we need to do the opposite of the last paragraph on heat exhaustion, and try to gently re-warm them. This could mean giving them your jacket or sweater and getting them next to a fire or someplace warmer. If they are wearing wet clothes, make sure you replace them with something dry. Wearing wet clothes is a surefire way of getting cold quickly and staying cold. This is why it's so important to dress correctly for the conditions, for example by wearing or carrying a waterproof jacket, and always carry spare warm clothes in case you get wet. If you can, give them a nice warm drink or some warm food. This will help to raise the body temperature and will certainly make the person feel much better.

Protection from Dangerous Animals

Now you have protected yourself from the weather conditions, it's time to think about what else could cause you harm out in the wilderness. Depending on what part of the world you are in, the threats can vary. For example, if you are living wild in remote parts of North America or Canada, then bears will be the most obvious threat. In other areas, it may be large cats such as mountain lions or tigers if you are in the sub-tropical jungle. Follow these simple rules of thumb to help you stay safe from large, dangerous animals:

1. Notice signs of animals moving near you by looking out for tracks and paw prints on the ground, and consider moving in the other direction.

2. Do not leave food or rubbish around your shelter, as bears, in particular, may be attracted by the delicious new smell and come closer to investigate.

3. Do not get in between a mother and its

young. Avoid getting close to a young cub, as the mother is usually close by and may think you're trying to harm her young.

4. Do not run! That is what prey would do, and a predator is hard-wired to chase fleeing prey. If you find yourself face to face with a large predator, try to maintain eye contact, whilst slowly walking backwards and away from the area.

Making a Spear: Sharpening the end of a long, straight stick with your knife is an easy way of making a great weapon for protection against anything that may want to hurt you. You can also use your spear as a throwing weapon if you find yourself searching for wild animals to kill and eat, such as rabbits and birds. Make sure the stick you choose is long enough, I would recommend it's at least your height in length. It also should be crafted from live wood and not a stick that has been picked up from the ground, as dead wood tends to snap too easily.

This chapter has covered the first priority of survival in protection. You now have a greater understanding of how to dress correctly in the outdoors, identify and treat major or minor injuries, and finally remain safe from predators and other dangerous wild animals. The next chapter will move on to explain the second priority of survival, signalling for help if lost and how to navigate using different methods in the wild.

Chapter Seven

Making a Shelter

Many different types of shelters can be built in the woods, depending on the kit we have with us and how long we intend to spend in it. Thinking back to our four priorities of survival, building a shelter sits right in the middle of *protection.* The aim is to provide some kind of physical protection from the weather and to give us a place to rest. The body needs rest so that it can continue to work hard for us. If we can't rest properly, the body will slowly weaken, and we are less able to think clearly and problem-solve. Shelters also can give us good protection from dangerous animals and insects. Imagine all of the insects, spiders, and other bugs that make their home in the leaves and debris on the ground, do you really want to be cuddling up to those at night time? A well-made and sturdy shelter made from logs could even help keep you a little safer from any bears who decide to come and investigate the sounds and smells you may be making in their backyard. In this chapter, we will talk about a few examples of shelters, how to build them, and what their main benefits and drawbacks are.

Picking a good location for a shelter

You may think that in the wilderness it's fine to pick any old spot to pitch your tent or build a shelter. This is not the case, and you should always take some time to choose a safe and suitable area. Flat, dry ground that is out of the wind and has some cover overhead is a great starting point for any shelter, but there are some other things you need to think about:

Protection From The Wind: Can you find an area that is sheltered from the wind and elements to help you stay warm and dry? It's important to stay out of the cold wind as much as possible. Wind chill makes your body cool down faster and will speed up the onset of hypothermia. Using hills, fallen trees or the sides of valleys can be helpful when looking for a good shelter site, as you should be able to use the features to stay out of the wind.

Flood Risk: On a dry and warm day it can be hard to imagine the area where you're stood to be in the middle of a raging torrent of water, gushing through the valley. But flash floods are quite common, and you must know this when planning your shelter. As water from heavy rainfall rushes downhill towards the low ground, it can leave natural channels in the earth. These will look like small dry river beds, with a bank on each side. Although they will look perfect to start building a shelter in, you must also think to yourself; 'what happens if there is a rainstorm whilst I'm resting here?' Would you be washed away in the blink of an eye? Am I in a bowl-shaped area that could flood with water when it rains? Much better to think about these things before you start to build.

Wildlife: Always make sure that you check out the area for signs of insects that could harm you. Making a bed that is close to an ant nest or a beehive full of stinging bees is not a great idea. Clear away leaves or brush from the ground to encourage small animals to politely relocate themselves to another part of the wood. Dark holes the size of your fist could be home to poisonous snakes or spiders and are best avoided. Be careful when moving any rocks, as many animals make a home under them so use gloves if you can. Always listen, as many dangerous animals such as rattlesnakes will make a noise to warn those around that they are not happy before they decide to bite. Insects also like to be close to water, in particular, mosquitoes are commonly found in wet areas and are a problem for anyone living in the wild.

Water: For any long-term survivor, having easy access to a water supply is super important. Therefore it makes sense that we build our camp or shelter close to the place where we will be heading to collect our water. If the water source is too far away, long daily trips will mean burning extra calories which we can't afford to do. On the other hand, insects and animals like to live near water which could be a problem. Larger predators will use the same water sources for their daily drinks, so look out for tracks and prints that may belong to something best avoided. We'll cover tracks and prints later in the book. We need a water supply close to our shelter but think carefully about some of the points in the wildlife section before choosing your shelter site.

Building Supplies: It is a good idea to have your shelter close to the materials you will use during the build. For example, piled-up branches of lush green pine needles are fantastic for using as a springy bed mattress, as they are strong and keep you away from the cold earth. They can also be used for thatching a roof on a natural shelter to keep you dry when it rains. So it makes sense to build your natural shelter somewhere close to lots of pine trees right? The same goes for logs, branches, leaves, or whatever may be useful to us when building a shelter. Similar to the water situation, it is all about saving energy and being smart if you want to live well in the outdoors. If you are planning to use a simple tarp shelter, you'll probably need to find two trees that are close enough together to tie a good ridge line.

Ready-Made Shelters: The extremely clever person will use what nature has already provided as part of their shelter. Caves can be used to get out of the bad weather and will provide some protection, but first make sure that nothing else has claimed the cave as it's home first. Bears and other large mammals can use caves as their own shelters, so throw something like a rock or a stick inside first to create some noise. You will know pretty quickly if there is anybody home and if you need to swiftly move elsewhere. Large fallen trees can also give some protection from the wind and rain, but again check for any dangers before jumping inside.

Do not spend too much time trying to find the 'perfect' area for your shelter. Perfect does not exist in the wild, and if you waste lots of time and energy looking then you risk making the situation worse. Be decisive and use your judgment to select an area that you think works. Remember, it just needs to be safe, not perfect.

Tarp Shelters

A tarp or shelter sheet is a vital piece of survival equipment, and should always be carried in your rucksack when exploring in the wilderness. Not only can it be used as a waterproof shelter if the weather turns nasty, but it can also be used to collect rainwater for drinking and even create a dry store to keep your precious tinder and kindling safe.

The A-Frame: Also known as the camp tent design, gives excellent protection from the wind and rain. The A-Frame is quick and simple to build, which is ideal if the weather turns bad unexpectedly. Although it has no ground sheet, once inside it has lots of room to move around and store things. The 45-degree sloping roof gives good protection from rainfall and wind. Trying to keep warm using a campfire can be difficult when inside the A-Frame, as it'll need to be placed outside and away from the sheet at one of the ends.

A simple A-Frame set up using a tarp.

To make an A-Frame tarp shelter:

1. Find two strong trees or solid objects which are at least chest height and around 6-10 feet apart.

2. Attach a long piece of cordage to the centre point of each side of the tarp.

3. Tie each side of the tarp to a tree or object as tightly as possible. The tarp will appear folded in half.

4. Attach more cordage to each corner of the tarp and pull each side outwards to make a

triangle shape. Use a few sticks as tent pegs to keep the sheet secure and tight.

The Lean-To: Again, very quick and simple to build, so ideal if you need shelter fast! This type of tarp shelter has a sloping roof that goes all the way down to the ground at the rear. You need to think about which direction the wind is coming from and make sure your shelter roof is facing that way, as the front of the shelter is very open and exposed. A great tarp shelter which is easy to build and enables you to have a campfire right alongside you if you're lying down inside.

To make the Lean To shelter:

1. Find two strong trees or solid objects that are at least chest height and around 6-10 feet apart.

2. Attach one edge of the tarp between the two trees at chest height and make sure it is tight.

3. Stake the bottom of the tarp into the ground at the back of the shelter, using sticks and stones to block any gaps.

Tents

If you have packed well, then the easiest way of making a shelter is to simply take out and build your tent. You can buy a pretty good tent from most outdoor stores, and they come in many different shapes and sizes. Some weigh only a few pounds and pack down to the size of a bottle of soda. Always use the same rules as before when picking a good site for your camp. It should be safe, level, protected from the weather, and have everything you need close by.

A dome tent

Tents work best when everything is nice and tight. Make sure that when you put the tent up, the flysheet on the outside is fitted properly and the guylines are tight like guitar strings. This will stop the tent from flapping around in the wind and also allow the water to run off quickly if it is raining. A tent with a built-in groundsheet is also useful to stop you from getting too cold and wet if you are sleeping on the floor. Ideally, though, you will have a comfy roll mat in your bag to sleep on top of which makes a huge difference.

Top Tip – if you lose or misplace a tent peg, then you can easily make a new one by sharpening a short stick with your knife and cutting a small notch at the other end.

Natural Shelters

If you need shelter but have no equipment with you, then your only option is to build a natural shelter. If you are carrying some simple cutting tools like a knife or a folding saw, then you can easily construct a home using what's around in nature. You will certainly burn more calories by making a natural shelter compared to a simple tarp shelter, but the finished product will be much superior. Choosing a shelter site that is close to young trees and bushy vegetation will be a huge help, and help you conserve as many calories during the build as possible. It will likely take one person around 1-2 hours of hard work to make a fairly decent natural shelter, but the more time you spend on it, the more water-tight and protective it will be.

Natural Lean-To with a heat reflector and wood rack

The Lean-To: Looks very similar to the tarp version, but uses branches and leaves thatched into a sloping roof. As you can see from the picture above, if you are willing to spend a good amount of time collecting and building, it can be quite homely. Adding features like a heat reflector in front of the fire will help you benefit the most from the warmth of your fire as you lie resting at night. A simple wood rack fitted to the front of the shelter means you can dry wood over your fire whilst covering the fire when it rains.....ge nius!

1. You need two strong trees which you can lay down in between, ideally with a little bit of extra room at your feet.

2. Cut a living branch that's about the width of your wrist and long enough to bridge to gap between the two trees, this is your crossbar.

3. Lean 8-10 strong branches against the cross-bar to make the framework for the roof.

4. Add leaves and vegetation to the framework to make a roof until you can no longer see daylight from underneath.

Thermal A-Frame: As the name suggests, this type of natural shelter is very good at keeping you warm. It's a little like a stretched-out igloo being smaller and lower to the ground than the Lean-To. But this means it takes less time to build and requires fewer building materials. It can also be built anywhere, as it is free-standing and doesn't require supporting trees. Now the downside – there is only room to lie down inside your shelter which is not great if you have jobs to do and want to be out of the rain.

1. Find a strong and straight branch or log that is roughly one and a half times your height in length, this is the ridge pole.

2. Make a triangle by leaning two shorter poles together to make the front entrance.

3. Rest the ridge pole on top of the triangle, with the other end dug firmly into the ground. The structure should stand up by itself.

4. Place shorter branches along the sides of the structure to make the ribs. This is the skeleton of your shelter.

5. Finally place a thick layer of leaves and other green vegetation such as moss on top of the ribs to make the sides of your shelter. You should be able to shuffle inside your new Thermal A-Frame with your head nearest the entrance.

Making a Bed

At nighttime, the ground can be very cold and if you lay down on it for too long, it will suck the heat right out of you. So a really clever way of keeping warm, especially at night when sleeping outside, is to make a nature bed which lifts you up and away from the ground. This will provide a barrier between you and the cold floor, which is called *separation*.

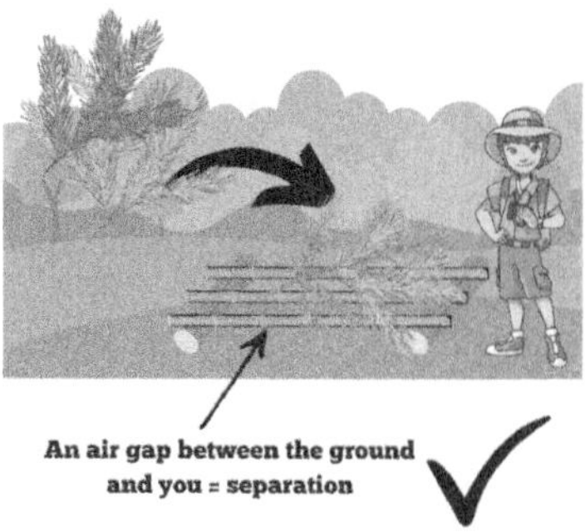

Making a pole bed: To lift you up and away from the coldness of the ground, a pole bed can be made in just a few minutes using easy-to-find materials. Top tip – make the bed just big enough for you to lay in, making anything larger is just a waste of time and energy:

1. Find two chunky logs which are about the same length as your arm.

2. Find or cut a few long, straight poles and lay them horizontally across the two logs. Four or five should be plenty.

3. Start laying lush green branches on top of the poles to make your mattress. Not exactly memory foam comfort, but it's better than nothing.

4. Your nature pole bed is now ready to use. You can even store firewood and supplies in the air gap underneath.

Chapter Eight

Signals and Navigation

Perhaps you're quite happy living out in nature, with no cell phone service or social media presence to worry about. Just an open wilderness to explore, hunt in, build shelter, and live contently inside your own perfect bubble. If this is the case, you don't need to be rescued or found by any search party. If this is you, and you are reading this book, I congratulate you. You are living a fantastic life, and I envy you a huge amount.

However, it could also be that you're reading this book to learn self-dependence and how to make great decisions to be rescued if you ever find yourself lost or isolated in a wilderness environment. This chapter will explain what you should do to give yourself the best chance of being rescued or getting to an area of safety. In the military, we call this 'promoting your own recovery'.

I'M LOST – What should I do?

Stop – Assess – Plan

As soon as you realize that you're probably lost just STOP. You must stop walking, as you are most likely just getting yourself more and more lost. Instead, now is the time to pause for a moment, take a big deep breath and ASSESS:

Does anyone know that I'm missing, and did they know where I was going?

It's always a good idea to tell a loved one where you are going and what time you expect to be home. This means that if you do not show up at the time you said, then somebody is aware that you may need help. They also know where you started from, which direction you were heading, and where you were trying to get to. This information is vitally important for any rescue party that is sent out to look for you and is the same as the 'overdue action' system that the Air Force uses if a plane fails to arrive at an airfield when it's supposed to.

Looking around, does anything look familiar, such as a river or mountain range in the distance?

We call these 'penny-droppers' and can help you work out which direction you're facing and where you might be on the map. It's always really important to study a map before heading out on any wild adventure, and you should always carry one with you.

Do not rely on your phone for Google Maps and other navigation apps to get you safely from A to B. Phones can easily be damaged, lost or drained of battery life. Now what?! This is where you confidently pull out the ordnance survey map and compass from your rucksack and begin working out where you are, before setting a bearing to a point of safety such as a road or populated area.

What equipment do I have with me that could be useful in helping others find me?

Now it's time to check your bag and take out anything which can help the situation. The best solution – is a phone with near full battery and service. Great, the GPS on your phone will show you on the map exactly where you are, and set a route on foot to the nearest place of safety. Maybe you're injured, exhausted or just frozen with fear. In that case, call the emergency services for the country you're in, or use 111 if you're not sure. This is the international emergency services number and will connect you with the right people. They can use the data from the phone call to find exactly where you are. Then all you need to do is sit tight and wait.

You're not that lucky, you have a phone but there is no service. Try getting to higher ground, if there is a hill nearby then climb to the top and try again. Still no service, OK what else do you have? Here are some useful items to pack whenever you plan a hike or wilderness adventure:

1. **Personal Locator Beacon (PLB)** – These can be bought from outdoor stores and are small electronic devices with a button which when pressed, sends a signal into space where satellites transmit your exact location to rescue services very quickly. This is the gold standard! Congratulations, give yourself a pat on the back for spending a little money just in case your worst day happened.

2. **A whistle** – 6 sharp, loud whistle blasts is the international distress signal and tells anyone nearby that you need some help. They should be able to find you using the sound of your whistle, so it's really important that you don't stop making noise until the rescue party reaches you.

3. **A map and compass** – In a while I will show you

how to use a map and compass to help figure out where you are and set a bearing so you know which way to travel to get back home. Just for now, make sure you have a backup to your phone the next time you head out on a trail.

4. **A small mirror** - This can be used to signal passing planes and helicopters and can be seen for many miles on a sunny day. Tilt and angle the mirror to bounce light first onto your hand, then aim your hand up to the aircraft and move your hand out of the way. This should be enough to catch the attention of the pilot who should investigate this strange bright light in the middle of nowhere. A big bonus too, mirrors don't need batteries so they will work forever. The only problem is they don't work so well at night time unless it's a clear night with a big bright moon, so pack a head torch and use that in the same way.

Get seen by a plane or helicopter:

ATTRACT, FIX and LEAD

Finding a person in a huge wilderness area can be like trying to find a needle in a haystack. Especially if there are thick, dense trees all around and a huge area to search. You need to take charge of the situation and help the rescue party by thinking smart and making yourself hard to miss. First, you need to 'ATTRACT' the attention of anyone who may be close enough to help. Then you're going to want to 'FIX' that attention so they want to investigate further. Then once you're at this stage, you need to 'LEAD' that person right into your location. Now you can breathe a huge sigh of relief, you have managed to get rescued.

Here are some great things you can do to attract the attention of the passing aeroplane or search party:

Ground To Air Signal (GTAS) - Find a large clear space in whatever terrain you are in. This is a great place to build a GTAS, which is a signal to passing aircraft that you need some help. You can use many different shapes and letters, such as SOS or a cross. I recommend you build a big V shape on the ground, as it has long, straight edges which always look out of place in nature which helps to catch the eye. Use bright colours wherever possible which are different from the ground to help it pop and be as eye-catching as possible. Ideally, you should stay close to your signal so that when the rescue team spots it and arrives to check it out, you are there. If you need to move away from it, then make sure you leave a message or note which tells rescuers which direction you are heading.

GTAS signals can be seen by aircraft flying overhead

Key things to remember:

- Build your signal in a clearing so it can be seen easily.
- Make obvious straight lines that look out of place
- Use bright, attention-grabbing colours.
- Stay close to your signal and wait for rescue

Tinsel Tree - Another great way of grabbing the attention of anybody who's out looking for you, is to hang shiny, reflective objects in nearby trees. This is known as making a tinsel tree, and it's kind of like when you help to decorate the Christmas tree at home each year, it needs to be bright and eye-catching. Now anybody who happens to pass close by will see something shining and glinting in the light and feel compelled to go and investigate it. That's exactly what we want as a survivor needing some help. Empty chocolate and chips wrappers are perfect for making tinsel trees.

The Signal Mirror - This can be the mirror from an eye makeup set or any shiny piece of metal in which you can see your face. The idea is to use the sun to shine a bright, eye-catching light in the direction of any low-flying aircraft or people in the distance. Depending on how big the mirror is, the signal can be seen up to 30 miles away. If you hear the sound of an aircraft, quickly head to a clearing in the woods and use your mirror to reflect sunlight in the direction of the sound. With any luck, the pilot or passengers will see a bright, glinting light coming from below and take a closer look.

Basic Compass and Map Skills

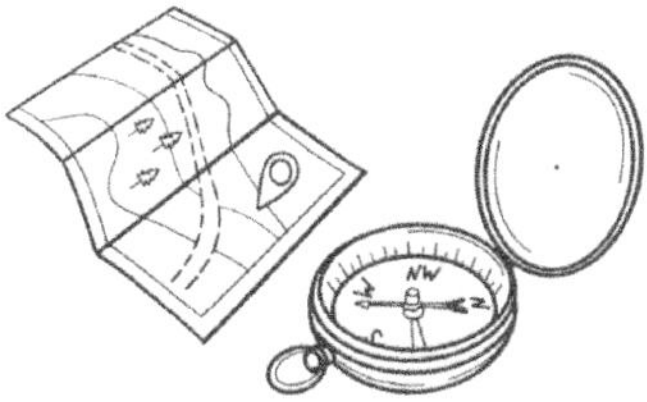

If you are someone who loves exploring the great outdoors, then you must learn how to use a compass and map correctly. Having a good sense of direction when you are out on a hike will mean that it's much less likely that you'll become lost. You should always pack a small compass and map whenever you are heading out on a hike. Exploring the beautiful outdoors on a nature hike is one of the most enjoyable things you can do, but you must remember to respect the dangers and pack things which you may need in an emergency.

A compass looks a little like a watch face when you

pick one up for the first time, as you'll see that it has lots of numbers and two hands. However, if you hold the compass flat in your hand and spin around slowly in a circle, you'll see that the magnetic hand always wants to point one way. This is because the magnetic field of the earth is always pulling the needle towards the direction of the magnetic north pole. Along with the north direction, the compass face also shows us east, south and west. These are known throughout the world as the 4 cardinal directions. **N**ever-**E**at-**S**hredded-**W**heat is one way to remember them, or **N**aughty-**E**lephant-**S**quirts-**W**ater is another.

To use the compass, hold it out in front of you with your palm facing up. Allow the north needle to settle, and then spin your entire body around slowly until the needle sits inside of the painted north arrow on the compass face. You are now facing north, pretty simple right? Now you have north figured out, you can easily work out where south is, as it's the opposite direction. East will be the direction to your right-hand side, and west is over to your left.

Put very simply, a map is just a flat picture of a

certain area. There are many different types of maps out there, from simple tourist guide maps to road maps, right up to highly detailed topographic maps. A map should always have the cardinal directions in one corner, often showing an arrow pointing to the north. Now that you understand how to use a compass, you'll be able to orientate the map correctly. This means that when you lay the map out flat, the north-directional arrow on the map is pointing exactly towards the magnetic north direction on your compass.

The final piece of the puzzle is to work out where you are on the map. The quickest and easiest way to do this is to look around in all directions and try to find any obvious points from your map; things like lakes, rivers, buildings and mountains. This will depend on how detailed your map is of course. Now you can use your map correctly, you can use it to help you find roads or built-up areas to get help.

Challenge Time – Make Your Own Compass

HOME MADE COMPASS

Step 1 - Take the needle gently rub the point with the magnet about 30 times.

Step 2 - Place the leaf in the cup of water so it floats on top.

Step 3 - Place the needle on top of the leaf, the needle should point to magnetic north!!

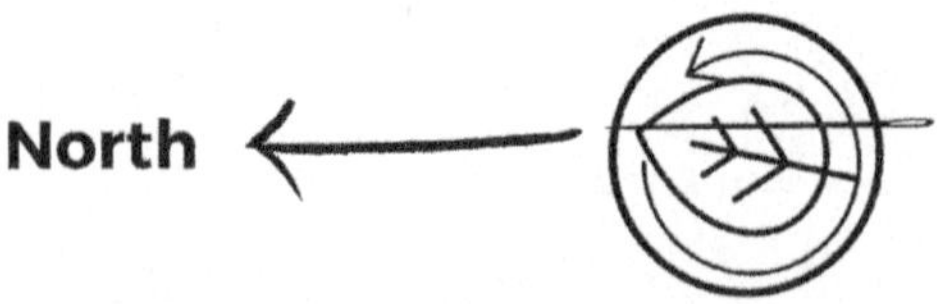

Astro Navigation

Sailors have used the stars to travel the world for thousands of years. It's a skill that can help you find your way, even without a map, compass or cell phone! A certain group of stars is called a constellation, and there are many in the sky. Luckily we only need to learn a couple to be able to navigate using the stars. These constellations will show you which direction north is, and from there you simply need to imagine the points on a compass and you can head in any direction you choose.

The Big Dipper:

Sometimes called 'The Plough', these stars form part of the huge constellation called Ursa Major. It looks a lot like a saucepan, with its long handle and bowl shape. Drawing an imaginary line through the two 'pointer' stars on the far edge leads you straight to Polaris, also called the North Star. Not the brightest star in the sky as some people believe, the North Star sits right over the north pole. Therefore if we face the North Star, then we are pointing true north.

Cassiopeia:

Just like The Big Dipper, this small constellation is really helpful when trying to find a direction. Cassiopeia is used to find the North Star, and it looks quite like the letter 'W' in the sky. I bet you have noticed this group of stars in the sky before, but perhaps never really thought too much of it. Well now you know it can be used to find the direction north, and is a great natural navigation tool.

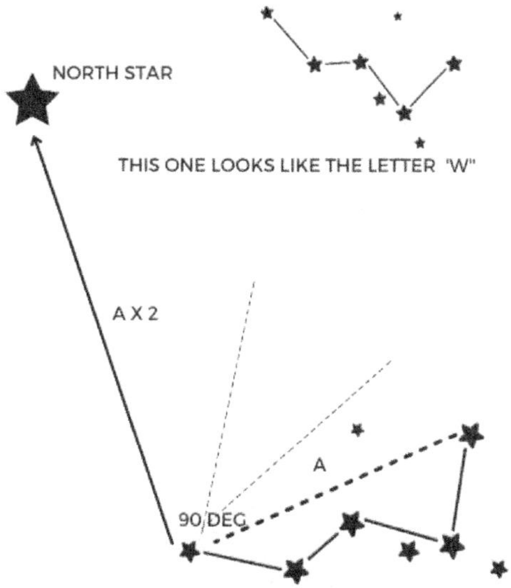

You have learnt two amazing constellations which can help you travel without using a compass. I challenge you to have a look for The Big Dipper and Cassiopeia the next time it's a clear night sky and see if you can pinpoint the North Star.

Chapter Nine

Finding Water To Drink

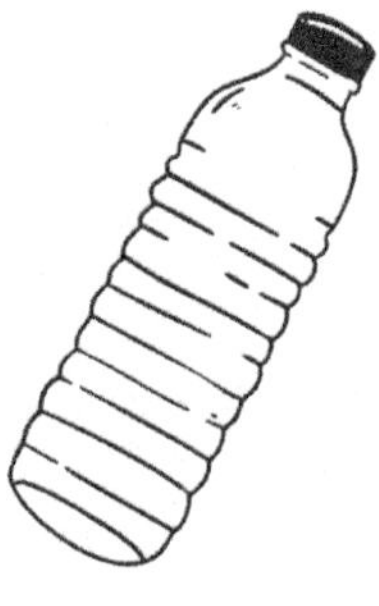

Earlier in this book I explained why water is such an important part of survival, and how the human body starts to decline if we don't get enough of it. It is normal to see your friends and family carrying bottles of water with them throughout the day, but how long does one bottle last? Under normal conditions, the body needs around 2-3 litres of water per day to work properly. At home and around school or work, it's easy to find clean, safe water to fill your bottle back up again once it runs dry. But out in the wilderness, this is not the case. Finding, sterilising and storing drinkable water takes time, effort and knowledge. In this chapter, you will learn how to find water sources in the wild and the best ways to make it safe to drink.

Searching for Water

Head downhill: Water always flows downhill, so it makes sense to start looking for it in the lowest areas. Walking down a hillside or valley will often lead you to either standing water, such as a pond or a lake. You may even be fortunate enough to find a river, as moving water sources are often cleaner and much safer to drink. Take a moment to study the shape of the land around you. Remember that water is pulled downhill by gravity and seeps towards the low areas. If you are high up, move downhill and you'll be drinking water in no time.

Look for the green: Like us, plants and trees depend on water for life. So you tend to find lots of lush plant life wherever there is a plentiful and year-round supply of water. Therefore, it makes sense to search in these greener areas for your water. It's almost like a big green, colourful arrow showing you where the earth is holding its water, ready for you to come and find.

Animal tracks and signs: As the local wildlife makes its daily commute to and from their favourite watering hole, over time they can create tiny flattened paths in the undergrowth. If you find such a path and it is moving downhill towards a green patch of ground, then it could be a great sign of water nearby. Insects love to be around water too. If you see swarms of mosquitoes or lots of bugs then you're probably close to a water supply.

Watch the birds: Around dusk and early in the morning, you may spot small birds travelling to and from water. On their way towards a water source, they usually fly quickly and in a straight line. After drinking, it's time to head back to their nest, but with a belly full of water you could see them making shorter hops between trees due to the extra weight.

Collecting Water

If you're not lucky enough to find an endless water supply such as a lake or a river, then you may need to get creative. Water is everywhere in nature, we just need to know where to look and how to collect it.

Catching rainwater: The shelter tarp which you have been sleeping under can also be used as a fantastic rain-catching device. All you have to do is make a flat roof type of shelter, and the rainwater will naturally pool in the centre of the fabric sheet, without the need for you to do anything except wait. Be careful, as the tarp fills with water it will become heavy, so you need to make sure that it is fastened well. If it is loose with weak supports, then it could break away and all of the water will be lost.

Transpiration bags: If you place a clear plastic bag

over the top of a bunch of green leaves and leave it for a day, a small amount of water will collect. This happens as the plant or tree, believing it is damaged, sends moisture to the affected area. Sunlight then causes this extra moisture to evaporate from the green leaves, and tiny droplets begin to collect on the inside of the plastic bag. The droplets will gather at the bottom of the bag if the plant or tree branch is held down towards the ground with string or rope. It's important to be certain that the plant you choose is not poisonous, as the water will harm us if we drink it.

Transpiration bag method

Dew harvesting: Dew is the layer of water droplets that form on grass and other surfaces, especially when it's a little cool. It happens because the surface temperature of the grass or plant is slightly colder than the air temperature. This causes water vapour gas in the air to condense and turn into a liquid, or water. This distilled water is safe to drink and can be collected. One way to do this is to wrap your ankles and legs in fabric and take a walk through some long grass. The fabric will absorb water and then you can wring it out into your bottle or tin. It is always best to filter and boil any water you collect, just in case you pick up more than just water droplets from the plants. Dew will also settle on a tarp or shelter sheet, and if you've ever stayed out overnight in a tent before, you'll have probably woken to find the outside of your tent to be soaking wet. Simply fold your sheet together to make a tunnel, and pour/brush the water droplets into a container.

Making Clean, Safe Water

Big Bubbles, No Troubles!

You have managed to find a good, reliable water supply but before you can drink it you must be sure it won't make you ill. Many different types of bacteria and parasites live in water, especially in the wild, so it's important to treat water before drinking it. This can be done in three different ways:

1. Use a filter to trap any nasties, something like an in-line filter fitted to your drinking bottle or system works great.

2. Putting a chemical into the water to neutralise anything harmful. Iodine or Chlorine-based tablets work well but leave an unpleasant aftertaste.

3. **Boiling** is the gold standard when making water safe, but can take time and effort. It will kill everything harmful though, so just remember 'Big Bubbles No Troubles'

Challenge Time – Make your own bottle filter

A bottle filter is easy to make and is a great way to filter out any large items from any water you have collected. Using different filtering layers, starting with the tightest net at the bottom and slowly getting larger, you can get rid of any small bugs, dirt, and anything else floating in there. Filtering water this way does not make it safe to drink, and it would need to be boiled or treated properly before you can enjoy it.

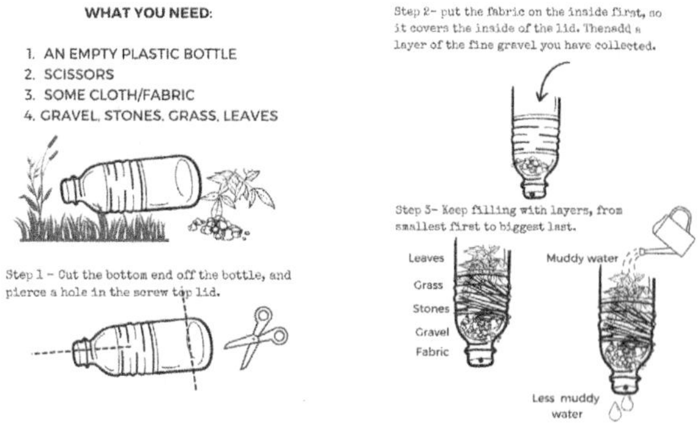

Chapter Ten

Foraging Wild Food

Food is the fourth and final priority for an off-grid survivor, as our bodies can last several days, even weeks without any food. This is possible because the human body can store energy as fat, which can be used to fuel us in an emergency if no food is available. As a species, this has been an important part of our evolution. Our ancestors in prehistoric times would have often gone days between eating a good meal, as some hunts would have been successful, whilst others were not. With no cave refrigerators or freezers to keep food, we had to become good at storing the energy in our bodies instead.

Plants

The easiest type of food to catch is the type that doesn't try to run away from you. If you know what you're looking for, then foraging plants does not take much energy or time. Plants can provide us with lots of important vitamins and minerals, which help us stay fit and healthy. Many plants can be used as medicine to treat infections or soothe insect bites or stings. The key is to have a good knowledge of which plants we can eat, and which plants we can not. There are lots of 'normal-looking' plants all around us which are very poisonous, and if eaten would kill a person within the hour. The number 1 rule when foraging for plants in the wild is to only eat something if you are **100% positive** that it's safe. Not 90% or 99%, you must be absolutely 100% certain, as your life depends on it.

Here are some easy-to-identify plants that are safe to eat, see if you can spot some of them on your next woodland walk:

Pennywort

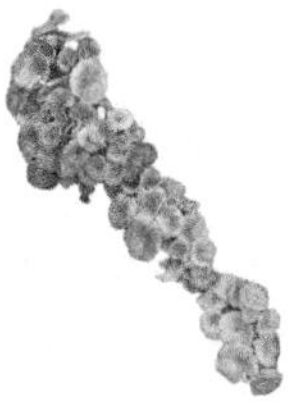

- **Edible Parts** – Leaves
- **Foraging Season** – Early spring to autumn
- **How To Spot Them** – Found in old stone walls and rocky areas, their green round circular leaves look like a belly button and are sometimes called naval wort.
- **How To Eat Them** – Great to pick and have as a snack, or take them home for a salad later. They taste quite like cucumber and are quite succulent.

Wood Sorrel

- **Edible Parts** – The leaves, stems and flowers are all good to eat on this tasty plant. This is my favourite find whenever I'm out looking for wild foods, as they taste great.

- **Foraging Season** – All year round

- **How To Spot Them** – The leaves have 3 green heart-shaped leaflets, which fold closed at night and when it's cold. They often grow in ancient woodlands, where the big, mature trees can offer plenty of shade and protection from any bad weather.

- **How To Eat Them** – The leaves and stems can be eaten straight away and taste like apple peel. The white flowers can also be eaten and taste a little sweeter. They contain oxalic acid which gives a sharp, tangy taste, but can also cause kidney problems if eaten in large amounts so be careful.

Ribwort Plantain

- **Edible Parts** – Leaves and flower buds
- **Foraging Season** – All year round
- **How To Sport Them** – Long green oval-shaped leaves have a 'ribbed' or striped appearance. The flower head is long and thin like a finger and grows from the stem.
- **How To Eat Them** – Pick the flower buds and nibble, they taste like mushrooms. The leaves have quite a bitter taste, but they are a superfood and full of health benefits!

Blackberries

- **Edible Parts** – Berries and young leaves
- **Foraging Season** – Late summer into autumn
- **How To Spot Them** – Bramble stems are very thorny, like tripwires in the undergrowth. The white flowers become juicy blackberries as we move through the summer. They look quite similar to raspberries but are darker in colour.
- **How To Eat Them** – The berries can be picked and eaten raw to provide an instant fix of sugar. For long-term survival, they can be collected to make a tasty and energy-rich jam.

Wild Strawberries

- **Edible Parts** – Red fruits hanging from the stems

- **Foraging Season** – Late spring into late summer

- **How To Spot Them** – The white flowers have 5 petals, and the fruit is red when ripe with seeds on the outside. The green leaves have a serrated edge to them like teeth on a saw.

- **How To Eat Them** – The red berries can be picked and eaten to give a feel-good boost of sugar, and as we all know strawberries taste fantastic.

Nuts

Trekking through most woodland and forest areas you will normally see several trees which grow edible nuts. Nuts are a fantastic survival food as they contain fats, and as we know from a previous chapter in the book, fats can provide lots of calories or energy. The fat in nuts is also unsaturated, which means it's healthier than other fats you'd find in processed foods like chips and burgers for example.

Nuts generally come wrapped inside a protective outer shell, usually with sharp thorns or tough husks. This protective shell makes them more difficult snacks for any local wildlife such as squirrels and raccoons. So any nuts you find in the wild, be prepared to smash open or tear the outer shell before you can enjoy the reward inside. Another problem with nuts is that they are seasonal, and are only really available in the wild during the autumn and winter periods from September to February.

Here are some common nuts that you could find in the wild during those colder months:

Sweet Chestnuts: The nuts of the sweet chestnut

tree grow within tough green cases which have long, thin spines. As the name would suggest, the nuts have quite a sweet taste and are great roasted over an open fire.

Hazelnuts: In late summer and early autumn, these nuts are ripe and will fall to the ground from the hazel tree. The nut itself is inside a small hard shell, and you need to use a rock, or nutcracker if you happen to have one, to break it open and access the delicious nut inside.

Walnuts: These can be harvested in early autumn time and are super healthy. The 'fruits' of the walnut tree in the summer look like clusters of green oval-shaped pods. As they become ripe, the green case becomes brown and hard. The nut itself looks like a brain and is soft and sweet to eat.

Insects and Bugs

In lots of places in the world, eating insects and bugs is part of normal daily life. In fact, often they are seen as a delicacy or treats in the same way we see candy as a pleasant treat. Grasshoppers or Locusts have more protein than steak pound for pound. That means if you ate 8 ounces of locusts and 8 ounces of lean steak, you would get more protein from the dish of locusts. Remember that insects and bugs carry parasites and other nasty things, so make sure you cook them before eating where possible. But what types of insects can we eat, and what should we stay away from?

Good to eat:

- **Crickets, Grasshoppers, and Locusts** – are grass-fed and have a taste similar to popcorn when roasted over a fire. Simply remove the head and rear legs (those with barbs) and then push onto a sharpened twig. Toast over a flame for a few seconds, and then down the hatch!

- **Worms** – Easy to find and dig up out of the

ground. Imagine they are long pieces of moving spaghetti. The best way to eat them is to boil them in some water until they look see-through, this helps to kill any parasites.

- **Woodlice** – Sometimes called 'Land Shrimps', these tasty morsels have a faint seafood taste. They're easy to find and mainly live under stones and logs. Just the same as worms, boil them in water for a few minutes to kill any parasites and then enjoy.

- **Termites** - These live in old, rotting logs, and you must break apart the wood to find your dinner. Full of protein, termites live in large colonies. To eat them, collect handfuls and roast them in a metal pot until they are nice and crispy.

Things to stay away from:

- Anything brightly coloured is nature's way of saying 'Stay away from me, I'm poisonous'

- Hairy things

- Foul-smelling bugs

How to catch a bug:

The bottle trap is the easiest way to catch lots of bugs because once you have set the trap all you need to do is wait a while. If you have taken a plastic bottle of water out with you, be sure not to throw the bottle away once the water is gone. It can have many great uses in a survival situation, let's talk about one of them right now. To make a bug bottle trap, simply cut the bottle in half leaving the bottom half. Then dig a small hole in the mud, just big enough that the bottle fits snuggly inside with the top level with the earth. To attract some bugs, you can use bait and sugar works the best. If you have something sweet in your bag, put it in your mouth and suck it for a while. Then spit some of your saliva into the bottle trap, and after a while, the sweet scent will attract any nearby insects to fall into your bottle pit. Once inside, they will be unable to climb back out because of the steep, slippery sides of the plastic bottle. Pretty simple right, but very effective, give it a try.

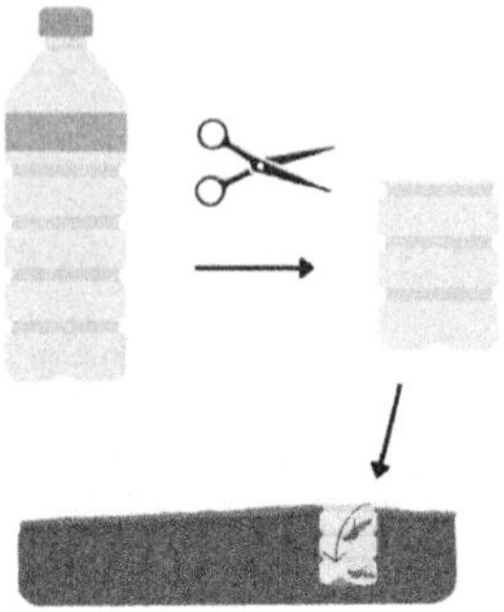

End of Chapter Quiz

Write down your answers in pencil, then check in the back of the book to see if you're correct:

Can you name 3 edible plants you could find in the wild that are safe to eat?

1.

2.

3.

How should you prepare worms, before you can eat them?

What is the Number 1 rule when foraging wild plants to eat?

Great work, you are smashing this book out of the park. You now know some foods that you can find out in the wild. Nature will always provide, we just need to understand what to look for. Let's move on to the next chapter, as every day should be a learning day.

Chapter Eleven

Setting Animal Traps

To survive long-term in the wilderness, you will eventually need to find a food source with more calories than just plants and bugs. If you sit quietly by your shelter for long enough, you will start to notice animal life all around you. From the peaceful chirps of birdsong in the trees to playful squirrels rustling branches in the distance, the forest is alive with potential food opportunities. The ripples on the surface of the slow-moving river at the bottom of the valley, are most likely fish happily going about their day. Now you need to learn how to catch them, prepare them, and of course eat them.

Fish

> Give a man a fish, and you feed him for a day, but show him how to fish, and you feed him for a lifetime.
>
> Lao Tsu

Fish are a fantastic survival food, as they contain lots of protein and healthy fats like Omega Oils which are great for your health. If you have the skills, you can easily get by eating fish for a long time. When putting together a survival tin, I would always include a simple fishing kit in there as they take up very little space. All you need is a length of fishing line coiled up, a packet of pre-tied hooks, sinker weights, and some feathered lures.

Using night lines:

Fish like to eat early in the morning as the sun is rising, or in the evening as the sun is setting. These are the best times to go out and try to catch a fish. It is a good idea to set a night line in the river or lake just before dusk, leaving it there until the morning when you can go and check to see if you've managed to catch anything. This is *passive* and allows you to get on with other important things like gathering firewood and fetching water, instead of being stuck next to the river bank waiting to hook a fish.

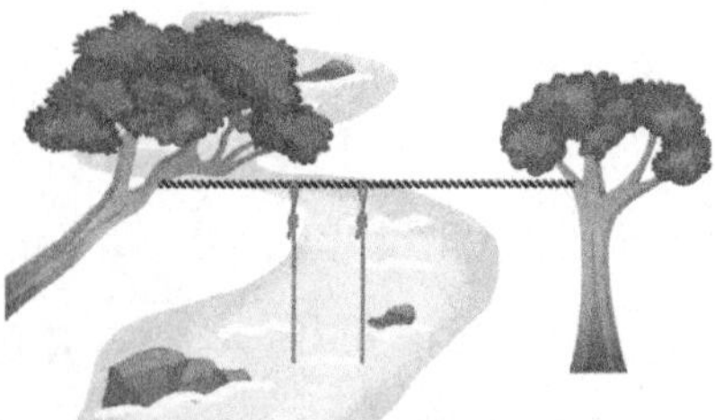

The best way to set night lines over a stream or river

is to tie some cord so that it stretches right across from one side to the other about 3 feet above the surface of the water. Then, using a lark's head knot attach your fishing line so that the hook is in the water. In moving water like a river, you'll want to fish on the surface using a feather or light bait. In still water like a lake, it may be best to try sinking the bait down lower using your sinker weights.

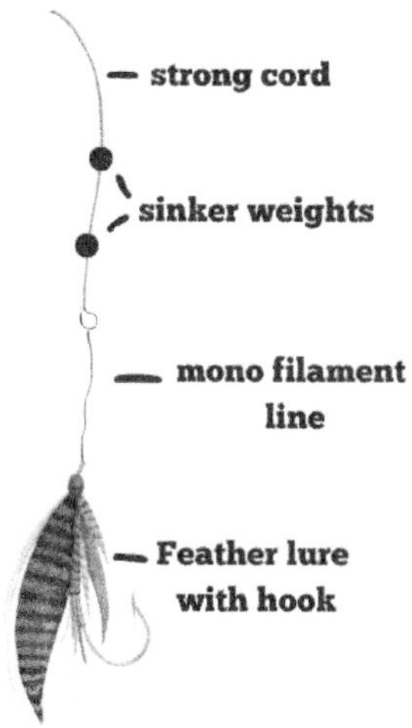

How to prepare a fish to eat:

When you catch a fish from a freshwater source such as a river or lake, you will need to cook it before you can eat it. This will stop you from getting ill if the fish is carrying any parasites or diseases. To do this, you need to first purge any poo out of the fish by running the back of your knife up along its belly towards the 'butt-end'. Now you need to gut the fish by carefully cutting the skin from the butt up towards the throat, before pulling out the insides with your fingers. It's a bit gross the first time you do it, but after that, it's pretty easy. Rinse out the fish in some water and then you're ready to cook it. The easiest way is to cut the fish into pieces and boil it in some water, that way you do not waste any of the goodness. Another way is to grill the fish over a fire by pushing the fish onto a sharp stick and toasting it in the same way you would a marshmallow.

Birds and Forest Animals

Without a river or lake nearby, fish is off the menu. So what other things living in the wilderness can we catch and eat? The list is long, we have already spoken about insects and bugs but they don't provide us with much energy. Here are a few other things that a skilled off-grid kid may be able to feast on:

- Squirrels

- Grouse
- Rabbits
- Turkeys
- Deer
- Rodents and raccoons
- Lizards

Now I accept that the list above does not sound very appetising right now. But imagine that you have gone a few days without any food, I'd bet that the thought of some grilled squirrel would quickly get your mouth watering. The problem is not going to be eating them, it's how you catch them in the first place. A rule of thumb is that you probably need to set around 15 traps, just for 1 of them to work. This means you need to remain calm and patient as it could take some time before you manage to snag your first meal especially when new to trapping animals. Eventually, you will work out what works for you and stick with this winning design. **Snares and deadfall traps** are two methods of trapping animals, let's discuss each one in a little more detail;

Snares:

Another useful item to have in your survival tin for any wilderness adventure is some snare wire. A snare is basically a running loop in some wire that works a bit like a cowboy's lasso. When the animal steps into the loop and pulls, it becomes tighter and tighter and normally traps the animal's leg or body. The other end of the snare is attached to something solid, so now the animal is stuck there. This simple type of snare trap is called a 'peg snare' and it can be quite effective.

So where are you going to place your peg snare trap? You will need to use your best observation skills and look closely for tiny tracks in the ground, caused by a rabbit or other animal as it makes its way each day to a watering hole or to its home. These tracks or 'signs of life' are great places to put a snare, as you can be confident that an animal is using that route often. Set up a peg snare, trying not to disturb the area too much, and then leave the area for a day or two. If your luck is in, you could have a furry surprise waiting for you on your return.

Deadfall Traps:

Here you use a heavy rock or log to squash the unsuspecting animal as they come close to investigate the bait you have laid. You can make a great deadfall trap using only materials that are already in the wilderness. For example, a Y-shaped twig, some berries for bait, and a heavy rock can be made into an excellent deadfall trap in just a few minutes. This means that you can set lots of these traps up around the area, remember the rule of thumb……15 to 1!!

There are more complex types of deadfall traps out there, and I would encourage you to search online to see the many different setups. Tribes in distant places like the Amazon rainforest or Australian bush have used clever forms of deadfall traps for thousands of years to catch food. Here are a few examples to get your research started:

- Paiute Trigger
- Figure 4 Deadfall Trap
- Split Stick Deadfall Trap

A good example of a Paiute Trigger in the desert using a big, heavy rock

I hope you found this chapter on animal traps useful, and are now excited to get outside a build your very own working trap to test in the wild. Remember, you should be respectful and thankful to any animal that gives its life to feed you when surviving or living off-grid.

Chapter Twelve

How to Survive in a Desert

When you think of a desert, like most people you're probably imagining sand dunes, extreme heat and maybe camels. But there are different types of deserts throughout the globe, each with its own characteristics and challenges. In Latin, the word desert means 'land that has been abandoned and left to waste'. With temperatures as high as 50 degrees centigrade, it is easy to see why very few people, animals and plant life are able to live in desert regions.

Let's now apply our knowledge of the **Priorities of Survival** to a desert area:

Protection: During the daytime, it is vital that you escape the heat of the sun and find some shade. You can make a shelter using a tarp sheet and using your hands to dig down into the soft ground to help keep you cool. Simply digging a hole which is around 30 cm deep will give you a 10-15 deg cooler area than at ground level.

If you are planning to move on foot, then avoid doing this when the sun is high in the sky. To protect yourself from heat stroke, dehydration and sunburn, you should only move when the sun is low or ideally at nighttime when it is coolest.

Be sure to cover your head with some a thin shirt or piece of fabric to help protect you from overheating. Desert tribes use a type of scarf called a *shemagh* to cover their head and face when moving through the desert, protecting them from the harsh sun.

Location: As few trees grow in the desert, it is usually quite easy to be seen from the air by any passing aircraft that may be out looking for you. You can improve your chances of being seen if you use most of the things we spoke about in the earlier chapter on Location.

For example, if you have a mirror it can be used as an excellent signalling device during the day as quite often the sun is shining brightly. Also, most of the land around you is clear of trees so you can see many miles into the distance. A ground-to-air signal (GTAS) can be made using rocks, sticks and anything you can find to get a message to any passing aircraft that you need help.

Fire is very quick and easy to make in the desert, as wood is mostly dry and fast burning. This makes using a signal fire a great option if you're trying to signal for help.

In the desert, the stars are very bright at night-time which makes navigation easier. If you know the general direction in which you need to travel, then use constellations like The Plough and Cassiopeia to point you towards the north star.

Water: This is without doubt the biggest problem you have in the desert. Water is absolutely essential to us if we want to remain alive and kicking, and the hot, dry conditions will quickly suck the moisture right out of you. The biggest tip I can offer you is this, 'ration your sweat'. Here the goal is to sweat as little as possible, as water in our body is just too precious to us. How can we sweat less? Resting in the shade during the day and travelling only at night when it's cooler is a great start.

It's very rare that you'll find water in a desert, but you could stumble on a small water hole especially if rain has fallen recently. Some plants like cactus contain water, but it is very hard to get to it without spending lots of time and energy chopping away at the tough, prickly outer shell.

Food: Remember, you can last many days without food so this should not be something you're wasting time and effort on straight away. Your best chance of food in a desert is by trapping and eating small rodents or lizards using the deadfall traps we went through in the last chapter. Of course, you would then want to cook them over a fire before eating them, so make sure your fire skills are on point too.

Chapter Thirteen

Make Your Own Emergency Survival Tin

The smartest people out there will always prepare for any situation. That means planning for the worst but hoping for the best. If you are heading off-grid either by yourself or with others, then you should always take with you a survival tin filled with useful items that can be used in an emergency. This survival tin does not need to be big or heavy, in fact, it can easily be the size of a small pencil case. This means that it can be carried in a pocket or a pouch in your rucksack, ready to arm you with everything you need to survive in the wilderness.

Failure to prepare is preparing to fail

Now what you decide to put inside your survival tin is entirely up to you. This chapter will give you a list of ideas but as an off-grid kid, you must work out which things are going to help the most. You should choose items for your survival tin that have multiple uses. For example, a fishing line and hook can be used to catch a fish, but also repair torn clothing or even stitch up a nasty cut on your leg.

Here is a list of items you may want to include in your emergency survival tin:

- **Lighter** – for making fire easily
- **Fishing kit** – food, sewing
- **Water purifying tablets** – making water safe

to drink

- **Small Compass** – finding direction
- **Compact mirror** – for signalling help
- **Swiss Army Knife** – cutting, sharpening, sawing, tweezers, carving
- **Energy Powder** – mix with water to fuel your body if without a food supply
- **Small Torch** – help to see at night, signal for help at night
- **Foil Blanket** – keep you warm, signal for help

These are just some good examples, and all deserve to make it into your survival tin. However, there are many other items which could also be useful, so have a really good think and start making your emergency survival tin today!

Chapter Fourteen

Animal Tracks

Can you tell the difference between a mountain lion print and a fox print? One of these animals is dangerous to us, and the other is a shy, timid creature that is no threat to us. If you can identify different animal tracks when exploring the wilderness, you will have a good idea of what animals are close by. Looking out for animal tracks is also very helpful if you are looking to hunt or trap wild game to eat.

When is a good time to spot tracks?

- **After the rain:** Just after it has rained is a great time to spot tracks, as the soft, muddy ground means prints are easily left by larger animals.
- **Snow and frost:** will also help you spot animal tracks quickly, especially snow that is fresh.
- **Near water:** Muddy banks of rivers and lakes are where you will find lots of different animal tracks, as they come down from the hills for a morning drink.

Here are some typical woodland animal tracks that you should be looking out for:

Image - https://www.wildliferemoval.com

Squirrels can be found in most places in the world, they are quite common. Their prints are usually between 1-2 inches long and look a little like outstretched hands.

Deer prints are very different, as they have hooves that split to form two toes. They are very common in woodland areas, with larger hoof prints belonging to the Elk and Moose.

Image - https://www.wildliferemoval.co m

A wolf print has four toes on each of their front and back feet, and the front feet are slightly larger than the back. Wolves are not that common anymore, as they have been hunted for many years. As they live in packs, when you see one set of wolf prints, you normally see quite a few more in the same area.

The Fox print is more oval, and the four toes are almost triangular. At only 2-3 inches in length, the prints of the fox are among the smallest of all canines. Foxes are very timid animals and will try to stay well away if they hear you coming.

Image - https://www.wildliferemoval.com

The Mountain Lion is a large cat, which means when they walk they can retract their claws to the inside of their toes. Canines (or dogs, like the wolf) cannot do this, which is why you will see claw marks on their prints. Prints of a Mountain Lion will be over 3 inches in length and width, around the size of your palm, so they are quite large. Although generally shy, they can be dangerous, so if you do see Mountain Lion tracks close by, then you should move with care.

A bear print is probably the largest print you'll see in the wilderness. They look very similar to human feet, with their five toes and long shape. You will see the sharp claw marks at the top of each toe, similar to the wolf tracks earlier. They are commonly found in the woodlands of the northern United States and Canada. Bears are certainly dangerous animals and should be avoided. If you spot fresh bear tracks nearby, then try to move away from that area and listen to what is around you. Often you will hear a bear making sounds or moving through the woodland before seeing it.

Learning animal tracks is a great skill for any Off Grid Kid who is moving through the wilderness. Challenge yourself and see how many types of animal prints you can learn before going on your next adventure. When you find a track, take a photo on your phone and then try to find out which animal it belongs to.

Chapter Fifteen

Real-Life Survival Stories

The 'real-life Lord of the Flies'

It's 1965, and in the small South Pacific island of Tonga, a group of school friends, aged between 12 and 15 – decided to 'borrow' a small fishing boat and take a little adventure. The six young boys, bored with school and studying, decided to take a boat for a joy ride around the nearby islands instead. For their special trip, they packed two small sacks of bananas, some coconuts, an old knife, and a gas burner for cooking. As they joked around in the warm sunshine, excited by the thought of their sailing trip and enjoying being out on the ocean, they grew tired and decided to take a nap. But as they woke, they were faced with terrifying windy, rough seas as a storm blew in from the west. Water crashed over their heads, and the boys clung on tight to whatever part of the small wooden boat they could to stop them being washed overboard. Eventually, the storm settled and the boys found themselves drifting out to sea with no way of sailing their vessel back home. For eight days they drifted across the now-calm water, with no food or water. To survive, they collected rainwater whenever it fell from the sky, using coconut halves like furry brown cups to store it.

On the eighth day of being marooned at sea, they luckily drifted onto a small, remote desert island. They made themselves at home and patiently waited to be rescued. And then waited, and waited some more. For an astonishing fifteen months, they survived on the desert island before help finally arrived.

In that time, they had made their own food garden where they grew fresh vegetables to eat, carved fallen logs in the forest so that they could collect rainwater, and even built a chicken coop where they kept live birds that they had caught to provide eggs and food.

Showing amazing teamwork and organization skills, they came up with shift patterns for important jobs like watching for passing aeroplanes or ships, gathering firewood, and tending to the birds and food garden. They were able to use their knowledge of the sea to catch fish from the shallow crystal clear waters around them. When the rescue party found the boys, although they were in good health they were missing their homes and family members terribly.

This story shows us once again that as a young person if you can learn life skills such as how to protect yourself from the conditions, find clean water, and gather food to eat when in the wild, it can pay off hugely if things go wrong.

How 4 kids survived alone in the jungle for 40 days

In 2023, a mother and 4 of her children boarded a small plane in Columbia to flee gang wars near their village on the outskirts of the Amazon Rainforest. They were hoping to start a new life in Bogota, the capital of Columbia. After 35 minutes in the air, and with thick, dense rainforest below them, the pilot sent out a 'Mayday' call over the radio. This is a distress call telling anyone listening that the plane was in difficulty and potentially about to crash land in the jungle. In this case, there was a problem with the small plane's single engine, and the pilot even reported on the radio that he was searching for a river so he could try and perform an emergency landing.

On board the damaged plane sat the pilot, another man, the mother of the four children, and the children themselves; aged 13, 9, 4, and a baby who was just 1 year old. Before they knew it, the plane was hurtling towards the ground, and it nose-dived through the jungle canopy and into the dark, leafy ground. Unfortunately, the pilot and the other male were killed immediately, with the children's mother badly injured and unable to move. By a miracle, the children were all able to free themselves from the twisted plane wreckage with only some minor cuts and bumps. After four days, the mother knew that she could not help her children, and bravely told the eldest child Lesly, 13, that they must leave her and go into the jungle to try and find some help.

Luckily for the children, the jungle was in its harvest season and there was lots of fruit nearby that they could find and eat. With their knowledge of the jungle, the children knew which fruits were safe to eat, and which weren't. We discussed the '100%-sure' rule earlier in the foraging wild foods chapter, and this made sure the children did not get sick. To protect their feet, the children made shoes from clothes that they were carrying, tying the fabric around their feet to help them move around the jungle floor without damaging their feet. Remember, protection is the first priority of survival and the children used clever thinking here to make sure they didn't become injured or hurt.

When the search party finally made it to the site of the plane crash after 16 days, they found remains of fruit and seeds on the ground, but the four children were nowhere to be seen. The rescuers instead saw four tiny sets of footprints heading in the direction of the thick, dark jungle.

For the next 14 days, over 150 Columbian soldiers with dogs teamed up with local people to track down the missing children. The soldiers used helicopters to drop food parcels into different places in the jungle, in the hope that the children may find them. They also dropped bright flares over the trees to help rescuers see during the night, but still, they could not find the brave, missing children. Something else that the rescue party tried was to play the voice of the children's grandmother on loudspeakers, telling the kids to stay in one place and not to worry. Can you imagine how scary it must have been for the children? All of this, while also caring for a tiny baby.

Eventually, a rescue dog called Wilson found the

four children and stayed there with them until the rest of the search party came. The young children had managed to survive an unbelievable 40 days alone in the Amazon rainforest, with no equipment, food, or water. Everything they drank, ate, and sheltered in came from the jungle. By this stage in their ordeal, the kids were extremely weak, tired, and hungry. With no place to land, the helicopter hovered above the jungle canopy and lifted each child one at a time using a winch rope, before taking them straight to the nearest hospital.

So how did these four brave kids survive all alone in the jungle for 40 days? A place where it rains hard for 16 hours each day, dangerous animals lurk in the darkness, and poisonous plants and insects wait to sting and bite. Well, experts believe it is down to their brilliant knowledge of jungle living and how they can rely on themselves to cope in tough situations. Life in remote Columbia is not easy, and for a kid growing up here is very different from a kid growing up in a city. Children here learn early how to look after themselves and younger members of their family, with skills like how to safely find and catch food and recognize the jungle threats, learned before most of us in the developed world can tie our shoelaces. The

General who led the search party put their amazing survival down to 3 main points:

1. Their wish to stay alive and not give up was impressive. For any survivor, this is the most important thing.

2. They are children who were used to living in harmony with the jungle.

3. They knew the jungle well and understood most of the problems they would need to face.

Amazingly, after 40 days alone in the Amazonian jungle, and other than being very weak and hungry, all four kids made a complete recovery. So it just goes to show that even in the most challenging times, the human spirit and a strong mindset will help you to overcome anything.

These are just two real-life tales of extraordinary kids who have the skills and knowledge to survive and live a completely ‘off-grid life’, and there are many, many more examples I could have chosen. Think back to what you have learned so far in this book, how would you deal with the situation that the impressive children in our two stories were faced with?

Chapter Sixteen

Urban Survival

We class an urban environment as a built-up area with lots of people, for example, a city or a large town. For most of us, this is where we spend lots of our time, while at school, college, watching a sporting event, or just out buying food and clothes in shopping malls. Because urban areas are so large, we need ways to get around them quickly and easily, so they normally have great public transport services including buses, subways, and trains.

Walking around a large urban area, you'll see lots of high-rise buildings that seem to go up as high as you can see into the sky. For some people, this can feel quite uncomfortable and as if everything is right on top of you. This is normal, and some people just prefer to be able to see lots of wide open space around them. In a city, you may only be able to see a few hundred feet in front of you at any time, whereas in the wild we can often see many miles into the horizon, giving a tremendous feeling of freedom and space.

Being around lots of people can be a good thing, and if we need help with directions or something else, there is normally a uniformed public worker such as a police officer or security guard close by to ask for help. Urban areas are quite hectic, noisy places and you need to be aware of your surroundings at all times, especially near busy roads and intersections.

Survival in urban areas is very different from a survival situation in a wilderness area like a forest. If you walk around a city for just a few hours, you will probably see homeless people living on the streets. They are facing a survival situation every day, but it's not in a remote woodland or desert, it's on the streets and in the alleyways. In a town or city, it is quite easy to find what we need to satisfy our four main priorities – protection, location, water, and food. To keep warm when it's cold at night, it can be quite easy to search for and find items of clothing that have either been thrown away or dropped by someone. Shelter from the wind and rain can be found in disused buildings or under bridges, with drinking water from public fountains and outdoor taps available to remain hydrated. Many homeless people will search bins and doorways for perfectly edible food which has been thrown out, to keep their strength up. Unfortunately, instead of being concerned with bears and other dangerous animals, survivors of the street must be on guard from any other human beings who wish to do them harm. So you see, it does not matter what environment you are in, the four priorities of survival will always remain the same. If you get these right, then you will be just fine.

What to pack

Most people will take a bag with them if they are entering the city. In your rucksack, you should pack a few useful things that will help you get out of any problem you face:

1. **A cell phone:** Always have a means of quickly calling for help, whether that be your parents, guardians, or even the emergency services. Getting service in a city is not normally a problem, unlike when you're out in the wilderness.

2. **Waterproof Jacket:** I live in England and it rains a lot......and I mean a lot!, so I never leave home without wet weather protection. They pack down really small in your bag, and weigh hardly anything so why wouldn't you?! It should be at the top of your bag, or in an easy-to-reach side pouch so that you can grab it quickly.

3. **A small amount of cash:** If your cell phone becomes broken or lost, have another way of

making a call. That may be using a payphone on the street. If you don't have a bank card yet, you'll also need cash to pay for public transport, allowing you to get out of the city if needed.

4. **Bottle of water:** We've already spoken about the importance of being well-hydrated, and going just a few hours without a drink can reduce your level of alertness and concentration.

5. **Energy bar or snack:** Walking around miles of city streets takes up a lot of energy, so packing a high-calorie snack will help you stay focused for longer.

Have a plan

Always tell someone where you are going if travelling into a city or urban area by yourself. You should have a plan for where you're going, how long it will take, and what time you expect to be home again.

That way, if you are late back then someone will raise the alarm at home and probably try to contact you. Use the internet to figure out what buses and trains you need to use for your trip, how much they cost, and how often they run through the day. If staying out late, then make sure you know what time the final train or bus leaves the station that day. You do not want to miss the final bus of the day and find yourself stranded until the following morning.

Possible Danger Signs

Cities are great places to have fun, with so many cool things to see and do. Sometimes though, bad things can happen and we should be ready to deal with that. Here are some classic signs that you should look out for when moving around a big town or city, and what to do:

- **Loud bangs and people running:** This could be an explosion or some attack on the people in that area. The best thing you can do here is find a building to get inside and move as far away from the entrance as possible. Ideally, find a room with a door that can be locked, use your phone, and call for help. Remember the phrase Run-Hide-Tell, which means run away from the danger, find a great hiding place, and when it's safe call for help.

- **Strangers who want to talk to you:** Sometimes nice, friendly people who mean you no harm will chat with you in a city, but be on your guard and wary of strangers who seem a little too interested in you, and won't stop talking to you. If this happens, say something like 'I'm sorry, but I need to go now', or even something like 'My Mom is right over there, and she doesn't want me talking to strangers'. Anything that will let that person know, you want to be left alone. If they do not leave you alone, then ask a passing person to help you.

- **Speeding traffic:** If you need to walk or move close to a busy, fast road then be aware of your surroundings. If you are staring at your phone or chatting away with someone, you are distracted and not focused on the dangers around you. Each year, lots of people are hit by moving vehicles because they have stepped onto a road without looking or listening first, and usually, it's because they are distracted. If you need to check your phone, then stop moving, step away from the road, and do what you need to do. Do not try to do two things at once.

These are just a few basic guidelines on how you can safely enjoy the busy towns and cities where you live. You will find that everything in an urban area is fast-moving, hectic and noisy. Take your time to make a plan of what you need to do, then tell someone where you're going and what time you will be home. Stay alert to what's happening around you, and avoid becoming distracted when near busy roads.

Chapter Seventeen

Conclusion

You have reached the end of this book, and by now I am confident that you have the knowledge and mindset to tackle most situations head-on. The main feeling that I want you to take away from this book is one of **self-reliance**. This means possessing a deep-down confidence that if things go wrong, you can depend on yourself to know what to do and how to act. Parents, caregivers, and responsible adults will not always be there to make decisions for you.

You have the power to assess the problem, figure out what you need to do, and then make the right decision. After reading this book, I'm certain that you know more about wilderness survival than most of your friends and family.

You have learned the four main priorities for survival, which will help to give you a framework when planning what to do in an emergency. Firstly protection, do you need first aid? Is there anything around that might cause you harm? what about shelter and warmth? Your next priority is location, do you know where you are? what can you do to help a rescue party or searching aircraft find you? Finding safe drinking water is so important, and needs to be thought about before you start to feel the signs and symptoms of dehydration. Food is your least important priority, and as you now know, the human body can last many days and even a few weeks without food.

You have also read about survival in different environments such as the desert and urban areas like major towns and cities. Hopefully, you have been inspired by the amazing real-life survival stories of kids just like you, who used their wits and courage to survive against all odds.

IMPORTANT: Turn back to the beginning of this

book where you wrote down those two goals about what you wanted to get from this book. It's time to check to see if you have smashed both goals and if you haven't, then you need to take another look through the chapters of this book. Sometimes we need to read something once more before it settles into our mind and we fully understand it.

I do hope that you continue to feed your desire to learn about new wilderness survival skills, and go out and practice what you've learned. Aim to learn something new every single day, and keep making those small, regular deposits of knowledge and experience. As who knows, one day you may need to make a huge withdrawal....

Quiz Answers

Priorities of Survival

Write down the 4 Priorities of Survival:

Protection, Location, Water and Food

What is normal human body temperature?

_______37_____°C

How many calories per gram are in fat?

_______9_____Calories

Foraging Wild Food

Can you name 3 edible plants you could find in the wild that are safe to eat?

Dandelion, wood sorrel, plantain, blackberries,

hazelnuts, chestnuts, pennywort, gorse, so many to choose from……

How should you prepare worms, before you can eat them?

Boil them

What is the Number 1 rule when foraging wild plants to eat?

100% I.D check and certain we know it's safe before eating.

P.S – Please consider leaving an honest review after reading this book, it truly makes a difference to us.

Printed in Great Britain
by Amazon

37506884R00106